Cultural
INTELLIGENCE

Cultural
INTELLIGENCE

INTERCULTURAL PRESS
A Nicholas Brealey Publishing Company

BOSTON • LONDON

First published by Intercultural Press, a Nicholas Brealey Publishing Company, in 2004. For information, contact:

Intercultural Press, Inc.
a division of
Nicholas Brealey Publishing
20 Park Plaza, Suite 610
Boston, MA 02116, USA
Tel: (+) 617-523-3801
Fax: (+) 617-523-3708
www.interculturalpress.com

Nicholas Brealey Publishing
3–5 Spafield Street
Clerkenwell
London, EC1R 4QB, UK
Tel: +44-(0) 207-239-0360
Fax: +44-(0) 207-239-0370
www.nicholasbrealey.com

Printed in the United States of America

17 16 15 14   10 11 12 13 14 15

ISBN-13: 978-1-931930-00-0
ISBN-10: 1-931930-00-7

Library of Congress Cataloging-in-Publication Data
Peterson, Brooks
Cultural intelligence : a guide to working with people from other cultures / Brooks Peterson.
viii, 229 p. : ill. ; 23 cm.
Includes bibliographical references (p. [225]-229).
ISBN: 1931930007
1. Intercultural communication. 2. Cultural awareness. 3. Social intelligence. 4. Cross-cultural orientation. 5. Business communication—Cross-cultural studies. 6. Interpersonal communication—Cross-cultural studies. I. Title.
HM1211 .P47 2004
303.48/2 22   2004040720

Table of Contents

Acknowledgments

Numerous researchers, scholars, and writers in the cross-cultural field have identified and defined quite a number of important concepts. Although a general concept like *individualism* cannot be credited to just one person, I would like to acknowledge a small group of especially valuable contributors to the field: Nancy Adler, Richard Brislin, Edward T. Hall, Geert Hofstede, Florence Kluckhohn and Frederick Strodtbeck, Harry Triandis, and Fons Trompenaars.

This book was sparked by a series of articles, lectures, sketches, and materials I have used over the years with clients of Across Cultures and with my graduate students. My students from every corner of the globe have taught me more about culture than any formal research I have conducted or any books I have read, and I have certainly learned more from them than they have learned from me. A few of them have become good friends. To these friends I would especially say *obrigado* and *gracias*.

Also, I want to acknowledge the following individuals for their specific types of support:

Dr. Howard Williams, for noticing that no book like this existed and insisting that I should write it.

The late Dr. Chuck Bruning, for encouraging me over years of weekly meals to stick to writing various things, including this book.

Both my parents, for three formative personal experiences relevant to this book: for starting me down the path of studying French when I was young, for sponsoring my first international travel, and for modeling open-mindedness to other cultures by genuinely befriending and warmly hosting people from around the world when exposure to other cultures was not nearly as widespread as it is today.

Dr. David Bastien, for his support as friend and colleague as well as his creative expertise as a cross-culturalist. Thanks for your insight, Famous Dave.

Many thanks to the Intercultural Press team with whom I have had positive interactions without exception. Specifically, I want to thank editor Judy Carl-Hendrick for her wise and able editing that turned what I had naively thought was a complete manuscript into a real book. And without the support and positive negotiation of then-president of Intercultural Press Toby Frank, I would not have signed.

Introduction

Who Needs to Deal with Other Cultures?

In every industry, from health care to manufacturing, working professionals increasingly need to interact with people from other ethnic and national groups, at home and around the world. This is particularly true for the Western world. Workplace cross-cultural contact occurs in three venues: with immigrants and foreign co-workers at home, in international trade at home, and by working and living abroad.

People Interacting with Immigrants. Many more of us interact each year with immigrants who work in professional fields, executive positions, managerial and administrative positions, sales, precision production, repair, specialty and technical fields, crafts, manufacturing, farming, forestry, fishing, and service industries.

People Involved in Global Trade at Home. Although global trade may experience temporary slumps, just as the stock market does, worldwide exports have consistently increased in the last fifty years, whether measured by value, volume, or production.*

> **Even if you have never traveled abroad, get ready to mix with other cultures, because more immigrants each year come to live in your country.**

---

* Source: World Trade Organization report on exports from 1950–2000.

Also employees in fields from health care to high-tech manufacturing have ever-increasing numbers of clients, customers, and partners from other countries.

About 1 out of 5 American manufacturing jobs is tied directly to exports.

Interaction with these international counterparts directly affects productivity, customer satisfaction, legal compliance, and the business bottom line.

This book has been written to reach employees working and living in their home countries who need to deal with people from other cultures in a variety of professional situations: working together at home; communicating abroad via phone, fax, e-mail, or letter; hosting international visitors; and so forth.

People Living and Working Abroad. Expatriates typically relocate to an overseas country for two- or three-year assignments. Many others do not actually *live* full-time abroad but may routinely spend from one to six months on assignments in a series of countries (they may be in the Hong Kong office this quarter, the German office for a project next year, etc.). Still others frequently travel to a region combining several different cultures (e.g., a business trip covering East Asia or the Middle East). These trips may involve international mergers, sales, or contract negotiations.

I hope this book can be useful for people in all these scenarios, no matter the language or cultural setting of the destination and no matter the country of origin.

I'm Okay, You're Okay; Let's Work Together

Let's begin by contrasting two cultural groups: U.S. Americans and Japanese. U.S. culture grooms people from the time they are in school and even before to think creatively and take risks. They are encouraged to follow their star, color their coloring books differently from the other kids, show creativity in their homework, give unique presentations in class, and see the world their own way. Americans say, "The squeaky wheel gets the grease." All of these traits lead to a creative and productive society, and they are some of the reasons that one could legitimately say that the United States is a wonderful place.

> **Olive oil is wonderful; it's used for cooking, flavoring, etc. Water is wonderful; it's used for cooking, quenching thirst, etc. Each is great for its own purpose, but pour them together and you'll see that they don't naturally mix well. The same is true with regard to businesspeople from various cultures. They don't naturally mix well, but in fact they can—and often need to—coexist in the same recipe. Without either one, the recipe will fail.**

Outside the United States, the rules are different. I like to contrast Japan and the U.S. to illustrate cultural differences because the two countries contrast in so many ways.

You guessed it, I'm now going to propose that Japan is just as wonderful as the United States is. In Japan, however, young students are not taught to think for themselves. From the earliest age, Japanese students are taught to work together as a cohesive group.

Imagine this scene, which was described to me by an American in one of my workshops. While working as an expatriate in Japan, he observed his young daughter as she was studying in a Japanese school. The students were seated at a big, round table coloring in coloring books. First the children would look around at the others and point a finger at the part of the drawing each wanted to complete. With just a few glances, the whole group would quickly agree on which section to color. Then they would point at their box of colored pencils until they agreed on which color to use. Finally, everyone would fill in the same section using the same color. The resulting collection of almost identical drawings would, of course, be quite different from what you would see in a U.S. classroom, where children are encouraged to be different and not copy.

The Japanese know how to work together expertly; they say, "The goose that honks gets shot." The focus on not calling attention to oneself and on harmony and group cohesiveness has made Japan a manufacturing leader.

We are culturally groomed to think and behave in certain ways from the time we are babies, and most people are not aware of their own cultural programming. But this programming has a lifelong impact. The Japanese lean toward teams, and the Americans prefer focusing on individual initiative and accomplishment because that's the way each culture grooms its people from the age they are old enough to learn to color in coloring books and even before.

The United States and Japan have very different sets of strengths. Americans may have invented the automobile and the VCR, but it is from the Japanese that Americans can learn to manufacture such items with the highest quality standards.

> **We are culturally groomed to think and behave in certain ways from the time we are babies.**

Every country has different cultural programming that results in varied sets of strengths and weaknesses. Both common sense and global economic theory say that countries are better off working together and tapping into their various strengths. Yet I have seen problems in many companies while leading programs on international business and culture: strengths in one country often seem like weaknesses in another. The very traits that create successful businesspeople in the home country often make people from other nations nervous, confused, or even offended. Wherever you are from, your local style of doing business is likely to rub people from at least some other countries the wrong way.

This book is about how to enhance your international work skills no matter what the "flavor" of the clash is. Your style is okay, and so is theirs, whoever "they" are!

My hope is that readers of this book will learn about their own and others' styles in ways that will make the process of international interaction a less frustrating and more fruitful and enjoyable experience.

Why Cultures Fascinate Me

Here is Darwin's theory of evolution, as I understand it, boiled down to four sentences: Animals evolve different traits such as different colors, longer or shorter wings, or harder shells. They don't do it deliberately. Instead, the offspring with the best-adapted variations (such as a harder shell or stronger legs) survive. This has resulted in a fascinating variety of animals.

Biologists who understand the intricacies of animals and evolution much better than I do will please excuse my oversimplification. The idea I want to express here is that cultural differences seem to be the result of a kind of evolution. Both animals and humans evolve, but it seems to me that humans do it in some interestingly different ways.

We don't just evolve physically but also psychologically, socially, and intellectually. We don't have to wait from generation to generation to see change, either. It's not necessarily the weakest people who die; it's the weakest ideas. We are all aware how the strongest notions tend to surge ahead and dominate the scene quickly. Yes, change is rapid. No, the dominant ideas are not necessarily the best ones.

Unlike the evolution of animals, human evolution and identity can be deliberately influenced or maintained. Modern Australia was settled by people who deliberately chose to change. China is dominated by people who struggle to remain Chinese. We are who we are because we choose it. Our choices are institutionalized by laws, standards, and socialization. We are more than just two lizards meeting and checking one another out, acting on instinct. We have written rules and codes of behavior.

Our cultural traits don't merely help us deal with the elements better, like fish might evolve better bodies for gliding through the water with less drag. Our evolution (if I may be optimistic) helps us learn to deal with one another more effectively within and among cultures.

To laugh at other cultures or consider them ridiculous and inappropriate is like the turtle (with its slow metabolism and hard shell) looking up at the hummingbird (with its fast metabolism, long beak for reaching deep into flowers, and tiny wings) and ridiculing the hummingbird for how useless all that style is.

People develop and maintain their cultures for various reasons, and though it may not make sense to us, it is right for them. Whatever system or method they use to get through their lives is what they know to

Look at that weirdo down there! Doesn't he know thick shells and slow metabolisms are useless!?

be best. Remember this when you're frustrated with the Italian obsession with style; it's exactly what the Italians feel (and know!) they need. And they're right! If you're an Italian frustrated by all the rules and restrictions in Singapore, such as where you can and cannot walk, hyper-cleanliness, and order, then realize that those traits are what Singaporeans know to be the best way.

My thought is that each way of living, the evolution of each culture, makes perfect sense within that setting, and the varieties can be fascinating, not just frustrating. How dreadfully boring it would be to only ever look at one kind of flower or to only taste one flavor. Some people, however, do just that, they spend their whole lives tasting only one culture.

Me, I need to get out once in a while and see the amazing differences around the world. Yes, it's a hassle to live out of a suitcase (as I have done four times during the writing of this book), but once in a while I need a dip into a very different "pool." Sometimes when I visit a totally new and different country, I almost have the wondrous perspective of thinking I'm an alien from another planet discovering life on earth. And I only have to fly for a day or less for it to happen!

Globalization Charges Ever Forward

People who know my business—helping professionals understand other cultures—asked me out of concern if my consulting practice had dropped after the attacks on September 11, 2001.

What a question! Ironically, some people assumed that efforts toward international understanding should *stop* rather than intensify after September 11. But stopping globalization is about as easy as stopping a charging elephant with a feather. Understandably, patriotism, protectionism, and isolationism increase during times of upheaval or war, but in the big picture this has never been able to stop global interaction.

Please understand, I don't suggest that globalization for the sake of globalization is a good thing. And I recognize that there are movements opposing the spread of world trade, and specifically the American corporate domination of world markets. There are articulate voices in opposition to the unfair, unbalanced aspects of globalization and in

Stopping globalization is about as easy as stopping a charging elephant with a feather.

favor of promoting local, sustainable, and independent markets. I also acknowledge the antiglobalization movement and recognize the argument that the poor around the world can suffer in many ways because of global trade. I further recognize that there have been, are, and will continue to be articulate world leaders from countries that are allies and/or trade partners of the United States who voice opposition to American political influence and military presence. I am not blindly in favor of globalization at the cost of local economies and cultures.

So when I suggest that stopping globalization might be as easy as stopping a charging elephant with a feather, I don't mean to be flip and I don't mean to suggest that the "globalization elephant" should be able to charge wherever it pleases. What I hope to convey is that people around the world will inevitably need to interact with one another in more and more ways: professionally, diplomatically, economically, socially, and so forth. My hope is that those interactions can be the fairest possible and always mutually beneficial.

Overview of This Book

This is a book about culture basics, because you can't ignore the basics. Whether you're practicing judo or playing chess, you cannot afford to ignore the basic moves. If you do, you'll find yourself flat on your back or checkmated. The same applies to the culture side of daily work and life. If you ignore the importance of culture in international business, you can prepare to consider yourself "out of business."

> **Most people think "culture stuff" is a soft skill. This can be a serious mistake, with a negative impact on the business bottom line.**

My experience leading cross-cultural programs for corporate clients and teaching MBA students has convinced me that most people think (or perhaps secretly wish) that basic international cultural differences can indeed be ignored. Many people think "culture stuff" is an intuitive, soft skill that can simply be improvised on the spot.

What a huge mistake that is. It's like saying, "The Beatles hits were amazingly simple—just three-chord songs thrown together with a simple melody. I'm sure I could sit down and write a few platinum hits in an afternoon." I have a hunch some people may think the same about being a psychologist: "Yeah, yeah, I could make a great psychologist. It's just a question of listening to someone complain. All you have to be is a really good listener."

Actually, to be a successful musician requires skills with an instrument or voice, talent, lots of practice, drive, business and marketing acumen, persistence, luck, and so on. Similarly, a psychologist needs a solid grounding in the theory, methodology, and techniques of psychology to be a successful practitioner. It may be an amusing fantasy to think you could instantly be a music star or renowned psychologist, but you can't just "wing it" in either of these professions. Nor can you just wing it in work settings where international culture plays a role.

My aim in this book is to provide you with a reasonable framework for understanding culture, to offer you a practical definition of cultural intelligence, and, most importantly, to help you increase your cultural intelligence.

*Bah...Just relax and be yourself...
You'll do just fine in any culture!*

The book is divided into six parts, each of which deals with a basic question.

Part 1 asks, "What is culture?" and provides a basic framework for defining culture in a way that is meaningful to a wide range of employees, from business executives to hourly workers who interface with people from other cultures. *The focus is always on international culture, not on domestic cultural diversity issues relating to skin color, sexual orientation, gender, age, and so forth.* Such diversity issues are important, but they are not within the focus of this book.

Part 2 looks into the question of why awareness of culture is important to daily work and life. This is a book about culture for people who "get it" and who want to learn more. I did not write this book to convince the skeptics who downplay the importance of cultural differences (though you might want to slip this book in their office mailbox). *Cultural Intelligence* is for the people who know culture is important, who realize that international cultural issues affect their daily work, and who want to improve their awareness, understanding, and skills.

Part 3 asks the question, "What is cultural intelligence?" I define cultural intelligence and examine the skills and characteristics that people need to deal effectively with international clients, customers, business partners, and neighbors. If you want to increase your cultural intelligence, you need to first understand what it is so you can set your goal.

Part 4 explores the question of how you can apply cultural intelligence in everyday work and life. This part focuses on a range of work, management, strategy, and people issues including, but not limited to, how we make decisions, what our work style is, and how we relate to people in and out of the workplace. These are examples of important situations when interacting with people from other cultures.

Part 5 helps you answer the question, "What is your cultural style?" My experience in conducting programs with a variety of people from many regions of the world is that most people do not know their *own* cultural characteristics. Most people think they are "cultureless" because, after all, they are "home," where nothing seems unusual and where they speak their own native language without an accent. The fact is, everyone has an accent, and everyone has a culture that someone somewhere in the world thinks is "far away and exotic"! The process of increasing cultural awareness and competence involves *first learning about ourselves and then learning about others.*

Another goal of Part 5 is to answer some of the skeptics who reason that culture is not important because of the erroneous belief that the world is rapidly becoming (or has already become) homogenized, standardized.

Part 6 acknowledges that once you know a little more about your own cultural style and what cultural intelligence is, it's natural to want to ask, "How can I increase my cultural intelligence?" Part 6 answers this question by offering some practical suggestions for dealing more effectively with today's culturally mixed world.

The part finishes with a larger overall view by examining how certain cultural considerations can be incorporated into business decisions. I hope that by the end of the book, you will be able to find innovative ways to apply some of the book's concepts to company policies, human resources issues, customer service practices, everyday business decisions, and leadership principles.

The Focus and Tone of This Book

Most of the time I have spent outside my own country has been in Europe, Asia, and South America; naturally, I include stories and examples from countries in those regions. However, the focus of this book is not just one country or world region, so I also offer examples from a variety of other places that are major participants in today's global economy. The stories in this book are either firsthand accounts of my experience or those of clients I have worked with as an international business consultant.

A quick note on style: When discussing culture, there is a great risk of tossing around confusing "isms" and theories. I won't propose to you any new invented "isms" in this book, and the very few "isms" I

> **It's definitely possible to talk about "culture" without using confusing "isms" or jargon.**

do discuss will be for the purpose of simplifying and demystifying them. I have tried to keep my language simple and to focus on the practical. I have written this book in the same conversational style I use during presentations to clients or graduate school classes. I put commas or italics where I would naturally pause or put emphasis during speaking. I hope my non-American readers will feel comfortable with my informal, American style.

And on that note, just what is an American? Many around the world call residents of the United States *Americans,* and that's the term I use in this book. Of course, people from Chile to Canada are just as American, and they could (and some do) take offense at the thought that residents of the U.S. might be implying that they are the "real Americans." In response to this, those who are politically correct use "U.S.er" or the hyphenated "U.S.-American." I find these awkward, so I have used *American*—but I certainly mean no offense. I sometimes use the term *Westerner* to lump together Canadians and Americans and sometimes South Americans or Europeans. Sometimes simplification is useful; it's then that I'll refer to Westerners as distinguished from Middle Easterners, Asians, Africans, and so forth.

Improving Your Cultural Intelligence

I will assume that if you are reading this (or assigning it as required reading to others), you want to increase your (or their) cultural intelligence.

I strongly believe that once you've decided to learn something, the first step in the process is to build *awareness* and *knowledge*, and then (and probably only then) you can change your *behavior*—and that's done by practicing. The simple distinction I am making with regard to cultural intelligence is between "knowing about" something and actually "being able to do" something.

For example, imagine that you want to learn how to juggle. You go to the library and check out a book on juggling; you read about the history of juggling, the different types of juggling, how juggling influenced the development of the modern circus, how Neanderthal man began juggling with only one rock, and so on. If you're ever at a cocktail party and someone asks about juggling—wow, will you be a smash hit with all your awareness and knowledge! People may gather around you as you pour out your fascinating insights on juggling. But will you know how to juggle? No!

By my definition, in order to truly *learn* to juggle, you'll need to *do it*, not just learn about it, and this means you'll need to change the way you move. When you start out, you'll flail around, dropping the balls. You'll need to spend hours practicing until your muscle movements are so coordinated and precise that you can juggle effortlessly. When you've achieved this, when you've changed your *behavior*, you will have learned to juggle.

Of course it's really helpful if you can find someone to show you how to juggle first so you know what to work on. Otherwise you wouldn't even know how to begin. If someone simply and slowly shows you how to juggle, breaking down the basic steps of which ball to throw first and how to catch it, you won't have to *invent* juggling on your own, you'll just have to learn it.

I use this same model for culture learning. Very frequently my potential clients think in terms of purchasing a one-day or two-day culture workshop (and sadly, some think a ninety-minute "culture talk" will be enough). That's how training departments usually think and budget things. Sometimes people ask me, "What's the point of giving a *two-day* culture program to someone who's going to the Philippines for *three years*? How can they possibly prepare for three years of living in just two days!?" Well, it's true that a two-day program is a rather short time to learn about the entire Filipino culture, but my answer is that in those two days of learning, the participants will at least increase their *awareness* and know how they will need to change their *behavior* to be successful in the Philippines.

If an organization or company can or chooses to invest only a day or two of time and money to prepare their employees for dealing with cultural differences, then at the very minimum I want the employees to have a solid awareness of themselves as cultural beings, to know what differences they are likely to face, and to gain a little bit of knowledge about the target country or countries. Ideally they should have follow-up contact with me so I can confirm that they're "juggling" the cultural differences correctly, or, if not, so I can suggest a change or two that will set them on the right track.

Knowledge about Cultures (facts and cultural traits)
+ Awareness (of yourself and others)
+ Specific Skills (behaviors)
= Cultural Intelligence

As you strive to increase your cultural intelligence, I encourage you to focus on increasing your awareness (of yourself and others) as you increase your knowledge and become more skilled at practicing effective behaviors. As your skills increase, you will naturally gain more awareness through the process, to which you can add more knowledge, upon which you can build more skills, which will then lead to more awareness.... This learning process is much like climbing a ladder— hand over hand over hand, and step by step.

Part 1

What Is Culture?

What images first come to mind when I say "Japan"? Do you picture sumo wrestlers and samurai warriors? When you think of Mexico, do images of sombreros or piñatas pop into your head? It's natural for images like these to come to mind when we first think of other cultures.

But of course it's also necessary to think beyond these first images. Unfortunately, because the United States is geographically isolated, many Americans have found it unnecessary to develop a deeper understanding of other cultures. I say this is unfortunate because there are indeed profound differences among cultures around the world—and within each culture. In a shrinking world with ever increasing competition, Americans are finding they need to know more about other cultures to survive both at home and abroad.

Cultural intelligence is not a piñata game!

In fact, I suggest that interacting with people from around the world without knowing much about them is a bit like bashing away blindly at a piñata. Sadly, I see some international professionals doing the equivalent of fumbling and swinging around blindfolded like children swinging at a piñata. The target (the piñata) represents the international partners, clients, and customers; and the candy inside represents the windfall of profit that is hoped for in the event that it's possible to "strike it rich."

That said, I admit that it's fun to learn about surface-level things such as French cuisine, Italian painting, or Russian music. But obviously a little deeper knowledge of what's happening and a little more skill in interacting appropriately would be useful. So to sharpen our skills for dealing with people from other cultures, I propose we use coherent definitions and frameworks for understanding.

Defining Culture

After a few years of teaching grad students and professionals about culture, I've found that sometimes people are at a loss when it comes to actually defining the term. People seem to think culture is a rich and fascinating topic (and I agree it is!), but what is it really?

The first and most basic definition of culture that pops into people's heads often refers to a geographic location: the culture of a tribe, a city, the West Coast, the British Isles. All of these are possible ways of grouping people into a culture. With this approach, it's possible to take a bigger macroview (Asian culture, African culture, Western or Eastern culture) or a more precise microview (Greenwich Village culture versus Manhattan culture, or the culture of your in-laws).

This approach is a good start for defining culture, but culture is certainly based on something more than "place." Turning to a dictionary definition, we might read that culture is "The totality of socially transmitted behavior patterns, arts, beliefs, institutions, and all other products of human work and thought" and further, "these patterns, traits, and products considered as the expression of a particular period, class, community, or population: Edwardian culture; Japanese culture; the culture of poverty." *

---

* The *American Heritage Dictionary of the English Language*, Fourth Edition, 2000.

Dictionary definitions of culture can incorporate multiple elements such as history, common traits, geographical location, language, religion, race, hunting practices, music, agriculture, art (and the list goes on). If we build a definition of culture including multiple elements such as these, we can further consider culture to be what people think, what they do, or how they feel. We could also include insights based on elements of human psychology, sociology, or anthropology. In fact, the directions for defining culture seem limitless, and perfectly correct definitions of culture can be so varied that it's no wonder people can be at a loss to articulate just what culture is in a way that's meaningful specifically for a businessperson, for a hospital administrator, for a teacher, and so forth.

The problem with dictionary definitions of culture is that they may not really specify anything concrete and useable for professionals. The problem with defining culture using list upon list of categories and topics is that this can lead to the reader being overwhelmed.

Still, some starting point for defining culture is necessary and helpful. My own "dictionary-style" definition of culture, if I force myself to reduce it to one sentence, is as follows: "Culture is the relatively stable set of inner values and beliefs generally held by groups of people in countries or regions and the noticeable impact those values and beliefs have on the peoples' outward behaviors and environment."

Here in Part 1 I expand on various elements of my definition above. I briefly discuss whether cultures are stable or change over time. I propose frameworks for understanding culture-based values and beliefs. I touch on the problematic issue of generalizing about entire countries, and I use a few short cases to offer some examples of how inner values and attitudes can affect the outward behaviors professionals encounter in the workplace.

In order to define culture in a way relevant to yourself, to your company or organization, and to your own work and life situations, I recommend you pick and choose a few elements from the "dictionary definitions" you like, from my own definition above, from the various lists of "culture topics" suggested by varieties of other writers, and from your own experience and insights, then come up with your own definition.

Culture is a vast topic, and I see this as a good thing! Unfortunately, many people make the mistake of oversimplifying culture without really understanding it in a useful way, and others can be overwhelmed by its vast and sometimes nebulous complexity. To keep the process of defining culture as clear and simple as possible, yet still meaningful, I propose you start by organizing your thoughts according to broadly applicable culture analogies.

Culture Analogies

I will never suggest that there is only one right analogy to use or one right way to think about culture. I encourage people I work with to come up with their own models, metaphors, or analogies for describing it. What analogy would you use? Stop and think about it. How would you complete the sentence "Culture is like a _____"? If I asked you to draw a model for culture on a sheet of paper, what would you draw? Consider it a minute before you read on. What comes to mind?

When I ask people in my classes or workshops to draw an analogy to describe culture, they come up with a lot of creative answers. I have seen culture described and drawn as a rose, a hot dog, a spiderweb, a pizza, a toilet, clouds, a wheat field, a bathtub, a circus, a dog (complete with fleas), and so on. Other common analogies that Americans seem to like (and they're more appealing than a toilet) represent culture as a melting pot, salad bowl, tapestry, or mosaic.

A tree is another way to describe culture. For me, it's a good analogy because practically everyone from everywhere knows what a tree is. A tree has parts you see immediately, such as branches and leaves. But a tree also has more interesting aspects the closer and deeper you go: birds' nests, fruit, bark, trunk, rings inside the wood, termites—and the life-giving roots underground.

A tree probably makes a more workable analogy than pizza. Trees are formed over many years by the constant, slow impact of their environment (wind, rain, sunlight, nutrients) just as people are slowly formed (by family, diet, environment, education). Trees change from year to year (dropping their leaves, losing branches, and growing new ones), but they remain essentially the same tree over time. Cultures and individuals may also adopt ever-changing popular trends, but somehow they remain essentially the same over time. All trees need sunlight, air, and water just as all humans have basic needs such as food, shelter, and clothing, and other needs such as various relationships, a sense of work or personal purpose, and so forth. Yet a pine tree will always be different from a maple tree just as a Russian will always be different from an Argentinean. There are certainly other insights we could have about culture by using the tree analogy.

Even though I've never seen one up close, I most often like to describe culture as an iceberg. While everybody knows what a tree is, people from some places may not know what an iceberg is. Still, I find it to be a useful analogy because of one important element: an iceberg has a part you see and a part you don't. This analogy is commonly used among cross-culturalists, and 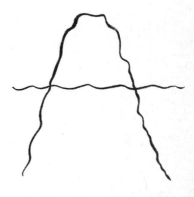 I like to use it with businesspeople because they can visualize what can happen if they ignore the much larger part of the iceberg that lies underwater—their business efforts may indeed crash and sink.

An important first distinction to make when examining any culture, therefore, is between the part you see ("tip-of-the-iceberg" or "above-the-waterline" culture) and the part you don't ("bottom-of-the-iceberg" or "under-the-water" culture).

Most businesspeople are eager to study the tip of the iceberg. This is understandable because it's the first thing people are aware of encountering when going to another culture. (Note: I didn't say it's the first thing people encounter, I said it's the first thing people *are aware of encountering*! As people learn more about the cultures they deal with, they may realize with the clarity of hindsight ways in which they were running into the bottom of the iceberg!) When you take an interest in another place, whether it's because you're going there or interacting with someone from there, the first questions that naturally pop into mind are along the lines of "What does it look like there?" or "Is it crowded?" or "What's the food like over there?" Our curiosity and attention are understandably first drawn to certain aspects of the respective cultures we deal with, such as French cuisine, the Egyptian pyramids, sumo wrestling, Chinese painting, Jamaican music, Chinese opera costumes, and so forth. These things can be fun (or delicious!) to learn about.

They can also be amusing, shocking, or perspective building. Usually the most off-putting things about other cultures are what we see at the tip of the iceberg: I was shocked, and amused, to see an elderly Asian man in the Hong Kong airport loudly clear his throat and, with a "graaaak" and a "patooey," eject a hearty glob of spit onto the nice new blue-gray airport carpeting. People from nearly everywhere are stunned at how fat many Americans are and surprised at how loudly they speak. The fact that Brazilians routinely

"Tip-of-the-iceberg" culture is anything you can perceive with your five senses:

- *Language*
- *Architecture*
- *Food*
- *Population*
- *Music*
- *Clothing*
- *Art and literature*
- *Pace of life*
- *Emotional display*
- *Gestures*
- *Leisure activities*
- *Eye contact*
- *Sports*

run red lights at night, even when right next to a police car, certainly is different from what a German might be used to. Americans are disgusted when the French smoke nonstop in enclosed public places, and the French cannot understand why Americans allow themselves to be controlled by smoking laws and low speed limits. South Americans are puzzled when everyone is herded out of American bars as the 1:00 A.M. closing time approaches, and many people around the world view American drinking-age laws as silly.

The tip of the iceberg can be interesting, but just as approximately 80 percent of an iceberg's mass is underwater, perhaps 80 percent of the important aspects of culture are also contained in the invisible and usually unconscious characteristics of culture.

Bottom-of-the-iceberg cultural concepts are extremely important for businesspeople to know. So let's take a closer look at the part of the iceberg that is under the water and why it's important.

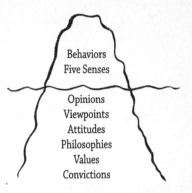

The under-the-water part of the iceberg represents what we can't perceive with the five senses (you just can't see or smell "time"; you can't taste "harmony"). The deeper you go toward the bottom of the iceberg, the more important the items are. For example, we may be able to change an opinion over the course of a five-minute conversation, but a value or conviction is far more entrenched, far longer lasting.

We could add more to this section of the iceberg, too: beliefs, assumptions, thoughts, hunches, and so forth.

I advise businesspeople to look for the cultural traits both at the tip of the iceberg *and* below the waterline. There are two main reasons for this.

Bottom-of-the-iceberg values determine the following:

- *Notions of time*
- *How the individual fits into society*
- *Beliefs about human nature*
- *Rules about relationships*
- *Importance of work*
- *Motivations for achievement*
- *Role of adults and children within the family*
- *Tolerance for change*
- *Expectation of macho behavior*
- *Importance of face, harmony*
- *Preference for leadership systems*
- *Communication styles*
- *Attitudes about men's/women's roles*
- *Preference for thinking style—linear or systemic*

First, the bottom of the iceberg is the foundation for what you see at the top. If you understand the underlying causes of why people behave the way they do, you are a little more likely to be able to anticipate how they may act or react in a variety of situations. For example, someone from a country where people prefer stronger leadership systems and more direction from superiors might (but is not guaranteed to) react better

21

Music,
Pace of life,
Architecture,
Sports, Literature
Language, Food, Gestures,
Clothing, Eye contact,
Population, Greetings,
Level of emotional display, Art
(...and many more)

Views about leaders
Tolerance for change
Assumptions about various relationships
Role of family
Comfort with risk
What motivates people in daily life
Importance of work and jobs
Beliefs about human nature
Attitudes about men's and women's roles
How the individual fits into society
Past, present, or future focus   (...and many more)

to clearer direction and closer supervision. Conversely, someone from a culture tending toward less structured leadership systems or a more relaxed supervisory style might want to be left alone to complete an assignment as he or she sees fit and not be micromanaged throughout a project. When someone does act or react a certain way, you are much more likely to be able to make sense of what is going on as it happens if you understand the "bottom of the iceberg" well. Neither of the two parts of the iceberg may be ignored; sadly, otherwise savvy professionals often ignore the underwater part of the iceberg.

The second reason for the importance of the lower four-fifths of the iceberg is that these principles apply to all cultures on earth. When you study and try to memorize a long list of facts and figures (and tip-of-the-iceberg information) about Italy, you can't apply this information on your business trip to Germany. However, you will be surprised at how many of the general principles you learn while studying the bottom of the "Italian iceberg" can be applied in some way to the German iceberg, or the to Saudi iceberg, even though these cultures are drastically different.

Cultural Values

For our purposes, probably the most useful category in the culture iceberg is that of values. I define *values* in a very specific and limited way when discussing culture: *"Cultural values are principles or qualities that a group of people will tend to see as good or right or worthwhile."*

For example, many people in a particular culture (let's call it "Culture A") may prefer to have deep friendships with only a few others—friendships that last a lifetime. Once these people become part of a group, they may identify themselves with that group for life. We could say these people hold certain values about relationships or about belonging to groups.

Others in another culture (let's call it "Culture B") might prefer the opposite: they might like to maintain a wide circle of acquaintances (acquaintances being not so close as friends) and rather than identifying themselves with one group over the long term, they might easily make the transition in and out of various groups as they go through phases of life. We could also say that the people in Culture B hold certain values about friendship or about belonging to groups.

Notice that my language above has been neutral: I said that people from Culture A and Culture B both hold "certain values."

Now let me move from neutral to positive: the values each group holds are different, but in each case they are fully appropriate for meeting the needs of the people within that group. In fact, on any given theme we might pick (like relationships or belonging to groups), the values seen in Culture A and Culture B might be polar opposites, but that certainly doesn't mean that one group should consider the other "valueless," nor that one group has it wrong and the other has it right. What they value and why may be completely different, but *both* groups have it perfectly right *within the context of their own culture*. (Recall the hummingbird and the turtle on page 6 of the Introduction!)

National culture groups tend to operate with a set of common values. Of course there are thousands upon thousands of exceptions in any culture, but still it's possible to make reasonably accurate statements (generalizations) about the values of a particular culture. For example, it's probably fair to say that Asians generally value respect, formality, status, and position. In contrast to this, Brits, Americans, Canadians, Australians, Scandinavians, and others tend to value directness (over respect or formality) and equality (over status or position).

But how does knowing about values help us to interact professionally with others? Can it help us know what to actually *do*? To answer this, let's look at the relationship between values and behaviors.

Values and Behaviors

One important caveat here is that *values are not always predictors of behavior*. That is, even if you know someone has certain values, you cannot necessarily predict what that person will actually *do* in certain situations.

For example, perhaps you've heard that Chinese children learn in school that one chopstick is easily snapped in half, but that it's impossible to break a handful at once. You may have studied the bottom of the Chinese iceberg a bit and know that your Chinese associates value group cohesiveness. Does this mean that when you work with your Chinese partners on a project next month, they will automatically form a cohesive team? Will they refrain from individual competition within that team? Will group cohesiveness really be put into practice?

Maybe and maybe not.

However, if you see your Chinese partners behaving as a group, such as involving the whole group in a decision that you would consider an individual decision or socializing after work in Chinese-only groups, then you might be able to explain this behavior in terms of bottom-of-the-iceberg values. If you see someone *behaving a certain way (especially if you see it happen repeatedly)* and you have an understanding of some of his or her culture-based values, you will also begin to see the reason (the value) behind the behavior.

Why can't we use our understanding of culture-based values to predict how people will behave? Because, as I said in the previous section, there are thousands of exceptions to the rule. Also there are great varieties of unpredictable elements that can influence every situation.

So while no one can predict even within his or her own culture what will happen in the future, knowing the bottom-of-the-iceberg values can help you improve your understanding of what is happening at any moment in an intercultural interaction, and it can help you significantly increase your chances of successful interaction in the future. If you know "what makes people tick" down at the level of values and if you can adjust your own behaviors to dovetail with theirs, you are much more likely to find comfortable, compatible, and fruitful ways of working together.

Big "C" versus Little "c" Culture Themes

In addition to distinguishing between the visible and invisible elements of culture, we can rank the level or importance of themes. For example, we can look at grand themes such as great authors or important historical movements. Or we can look at more minor themes such as current popular trends or news items. These major or minor themes are frequently called Big "C" or Little "c" culture.

The table below represents the intersection between Big "C," Little "c"/"invisible" and "visible" cultures. I recommend people study a variety of issues relating to all four areas of this table.

	Big "C" Culture *Classic or grand themes*	**Little "c" Culture** *Minor or common themes*
Invisible Culture *"Bottom of the iceberg"*	**Examples:** Core values, attitudes or beliefs, society's norms, legal foundations, assumptions, history, cognitive processes	**Examples:** Popular issues, opinions, viewpoints, preferences or tastes, certain knowledge (trivia, facts)
Visible Culture *"Tip of the iceberg"*	**Examples:** Architecture, geography, classic literature, presidents or political figures, classical music	**Examples:** Gestures, body posture, use of space, clothing style, food, hobbies, music, artwork

I don't mean for this table to be a complicated formula for considering culture. It just shows that there are various ways of thinking about cultures. Some people seem to think that the ultimate way to learn about a culture (e.g., French culture) is through reading literature (e.g., French literature) from a few hundred years ago. I've spent a lot of time in France and studied a lot of French literature. I still enjoy reading it, but I've never found French literature to be very useful for understanding the French. My point is that you shouldn't make the mistake of focusing on only one limited area when you begin learning about a culture. Pick and choose a variety of subjects to explore from all four quadrants of the table above.

Stereotypes versus Generalizations

The distinction between stereotypes and generalizations comes up in discussions in almost every cross-cultural program I deliver to clients. It's an ever-present issue because people are afraid to make generalizations and to use stereotypes, although we all do some (or plenty) of both.

Stereotypes

A stereotype is usually a negative statement made about a group of people (e.g., Mexicans). Stereotypes emerge when we apply one perception to an entire group. For example, we might know one Chinese man who is extremely quiet and shy and because of this, we conclude that all Chinese people are quiet and shy. (Incidentally,

My best friend's wife is Mexican.

how untrue this is of the Chinese, who can be enthusiastic, noisy, and boisterous! At the same time, respecting silence, saving face, and following protocol are useful for interacting with the Chinese.)

Because we are afraid to use stereotypes, we are often afraid to talk about culture groups (make generalizations) at all. I was once coaching an American couple relocating on assignment to Mexico City. The husband mentioned to me that they had a good friend who had married a

My Japanese sister-in-law certainly doesn't do things that way!

Mexican woman. He whispered *Mexican* as if it were an embarrassing or vulgar word to be avoided for some reason. Yes, it is true that some Americans have some pretty negative stereotypes about Mexicans and might therefore want to avoid the very word *Mexican*. One of the things I had to address in my sessions with them is that there is a whole country full of people who are as proud to be Mexican as that man was proud to be American and that it's perfectly acceptable to say "Mexican" at the top of your voice!

Positive stereotypes might not seem as damaging. An example of a positive stereotype is "Asians are good at math" or "Germans make wonderful engineers." The problem with positive stereotypes is that, like negative ones, they only paint a partial picture of the person you're dealing with and they may not be accurate. And they certainly no more describe all Asians or all Germans than my clients' negative stereotypes would apply to all Mexicans.

Generalizations

Generalizations, as I define them, are quite different from stereotypes (and more reliable). With generalizations, we look at a large number of people and we draw certain conclusions from what we see. For example, cross-cultural experts and professionals or businesspeople might study Venezuelans and/or live, work, and interact with dozens or hundreds of

Generalizations can help establish a rough map.

Venezuelans. After synthesizing all the available information (from surveys to personal experiences), it may be possible to make a few accurate, general statements about the culture. Venezuelans, as it happens, do indeed have a high expectation of macho behavior in their culture. And women's and men's roles in Venezuela are more distinct than in many other cultures. If you want to do business in Venezuela or with Venezuelans, you would need to know how these issues affect the workplace, product marketing, relationship building, decision-making style, negotiating, the choice of who represents a company in a negotiation, and so on.

There are exceptions to every rule, but generalizations that come from research and from the insights of informed international cultural experts and professionals allow us to paint a fairly accurate picture of how people in a given country are likely (but never guaranteed) to operate.

Do Cultures Change over Time?

As soon as we think we have somewhat of a grasp on how to describe various cultures, some people will point out that cultures change over time. And those people are right!

But yet another set of people will make the argument that cultures remain the same over time. They're right too!

Consider the westward-bound settlers in the United States in the 1800s, who *had* to be rugged individualists to embark on such hazardous journeys. Many Americans remain "rugged individualists" in many ways today. Yet the U.S. has changed more than a little since the 1800s!

We could answer both sets of people above by returning to our tree analogy. The trunk and basic form of the tree remain essentially

Cultures change daily!

the same over the years, but the leaves change color every season and are replaced every year, entire branches may break off and fall, and new ones grow. In spite of these changes, though, a willow is always a willow and a redwood remains a redwood. A maple tree remains a maple tree throughout its life, and we should always be able to tell fir trees from oak trees and identify them as different from one another.

Of course cultures change. But cultures also maintain certain traits over decades and centuries. We cannot escape these seemingly conflicting cultural forces and must adjust to them in order to be suc-

Cultures remain the same over centuries!

cessful. Big "C" culture themes may tend to remain the same over time, while Little "c" themes might be more prone to change over months and years. Japan is a good example of a culture that has changed drastically in some ways (more individualized, reduced loyalty to employers, etc.) in the last fifty years but that still holds to traditions and many cultural traits thousands of years old (harmony, face, hierarchy, etc.)

A simple way to meaningfully categorize the complex and ever-changing cultural phenomena we encounter is to focus on "general themes," which will be discussed for the rest of Part 1.

No matter what framework you use to define or analogize culture, an important distinction to make (and also a quick and simple one) is between what could be called "general themes" (themes that apply to the whole world) and "culture-specific themes" (concepts that apply to just one culture).

An example of a general theme is the issue of men's and women's roles. In some cultures men and women are expected to behave and to be treated equally; in other cultures, they are expected to be treated and to behave in distinct ways. Regardless of how we define a spectrum for understanding men's and women's roles, every culture on earth has men and women, so men's and women's issues are dealt with in some way. Every culture on earth also has young people and old people, and every culture has a way of viewing the past, present, and future. Issues relating to such themes are played out, with various degrees of importance, in boardrooms in Hong Kong as well as in tribal councils in the rainforest.

Examples of culture-specific themes are environmental activism, volunteerism, and wine making. Of course not every culture on earth engages in (or even knows or cares about) these.

I recommend first focusing on general themes, because a foundation of understanding about these cultural characteristics will help you deal with people from a variety of countries. Then it's important to "fill in the details" with culture-specific themes for the specific cultures you interact with. The next section proposes five basic scales for helping you make sense of culture-general themes.

Five Basic Culture Scales

If you run an Internet search using the word *culture*, you'll find thousands of returns—everything from articles on the bacteria culture living in the petri dishes in laboratories to lessons in art history and the meaning of impressionistic painting. You might even find something relevant to working and building better relationships across cultures.

If you search a little deeper, you will find a variety of researchers, writers, and scholars who have relevant ideas on what is important to consider about culture. But the experts don't exactly agree: One writer says that there are 13 things you must know about culture. Another scholar declares there are 72 crucial categories. Still another one claims there are 7, and yet a fourth one states there are 11 major themes you need to know. One of the best-known cross-cultural researchers initially settled on 4 critical themes, but later he added one more. And that person's main intellectual competitor, another well-known writer in the field, suggests there are 6 scales to consider.

The terms many cross-cultural experts use can be far from simple. Consider, for example, the terms *masculine* and *feminine*. They are commonly used words outside cross-cultural circles, but they may not help most professionals understand culture very much. For example, if someone tells me that U.S. culture is quite "masculine," should I puff out my chest and say, "Thank you! Uh...I'm not quite sure what you mean!" If that same person claims that Sweden leans strongly toward the "feminine," should Swedes be honored or offended? Is it bad for a country to be masculine or feminine? Hey, maybe Swedes might be "feeling in touch with their feminine side," whatever *that* means!

I don't mean to make light of a serious concept that many cross-culturalists find useful. The terms *masculine* and *feminine* do address

...but are Italian women "masculine?"

important culture concepts. Masculine cultures prefer greater separation between men's and women's roles, while feminine cultures tend toward equality.

The average person who deals daily with people from other cultures will probably not find these terms very insightful. In my work as a cross-cultural consultant and grad school professor, I've seen a lot of students and clients (and even other professors) confused by terms like these. What does it really mean to say Italians are masculine? Are Italian women masculine too? Does this sense of masculinity mean Italy is a work-driven society like Japan, which is also considered masculine? No, it doesn't. I've seen so many MBA students and executives stumped or misguided (or downright angered!) by the use of these terms in a cultural context that I do not recommend using them.

I don't think most people like to memorize terms like *universalism* or *particularism* either. The concepts behind these two terms are quite important and can be very useful in discussing business ethics issues: people from "universalistic" cultures feel that rules are rules and are not meant to be bent or broken; people from "particularistic" cultures find rules more flexible and consider exceptions to the rule ordinary. But I prefer to use simpler language.

What terms can we use, then, to meaningfully describe a framework for culture? Not only is there a wide variety of terms used to describe cultural dimensions, there is also a lot of overlap. As I mentioned in the Introduction, what one person calls "doing" versus "being," another calls "task" versus "relationship." Although the ideas behind these terms are not exactly the same, they share a lot in common.

A commonality of many such approaches is that they suggest sets of differences or sometimes opposite poles (like "black" on one extreme and "white" on the other). To show that there can be gray areas in between, a continuum between the two poles with a scale of zero to ten is helpful.

0	1	2	3	4	5	6	7	8	9	10

Black   **Gray Area**   **White**

Beware of oversimplification, however. The gray area in the scales is a reminder to avoid extremes when we describe cultures; it also suggests that there can be many nuances rather than an "either/or" approach that just looks at opposites.

For example, we can ask, *"Are the French individualistic (one extreme) or group oriented (the other extreme)?"* Most French people I ask this question of immediately respond, "Individualistic" and support their statement by referring to the French tendency to openly express their own unique opinions, the desire for privacy, and so forth. Still, France is a country with socialized

To those who say culture doesn't matter and we're really all the same, I say: A chicken and a buffalo are essentially the same thing too, aren't they? Both have tails and walk on land, and neither one runs backward very well. They're also about the same size if viewed from a certain perspective.

medicine and education, and the entire country moves like a herd to the French Riviera in August. So on a scale of 0–10, our individual/ group number for France would depend on whether we are talking about socialized medicine, French outspokenness, vacation habits, or a multitude of other issues. And are the French more or less individualistic than, say, the Australians? To answer that, we would need to be sure we were comparing the same aspects of individualism between the French and the Australians. And we would need to be mindful of the difference between *individualism* and *individuality* (a distinction I make later in this section).

The danger of assigning simple numbers to something as complex and nuanced as a cultural trait is that people will think there is an absolute and correct answer (Germany is 9.4, Saudi Arabia is 3.6). Actually, the only reason to assign such numbers is so that we can begin to make some reasonably accurate comparisons regarding the relative position of various cultures.

When we're talking about a specific theme (such as how aggressive people are in negotiation), one culture (such as the Philippines) might be toward the left end of a passive/aggressive scale at about 1 or 2, while one's own culture (such as the U.S.) might be toward the right at about 8 or 9, that is, quite aggressive. Filipino and U.S. negotiators then have some idea how to look for differences when they negotiate with each other.

0	1	2	3	4	5	6	7	8	9	10

←──→

Passive   **Assertive**   **Aggressive**
Negotiators   **Negotiators**   **Negotiators**

But remember this: Knowing a precise number for a culture or trying to determine an absolute, unchangeable position on the scale is not the point. The point is to know the elements that make up each scale and to determine the general position of a country on the scale.

And once again, it's important to remember where the generalization breaks down: If the "average Austrian" is supposedly at 4 on a given scale, you are guaranteed to find many exceptions, because of course the perfect prototype of the "average Austrian" doesn't exist.

At any rate, businesspeople need a way of understanding cultural differences that is simple, relevant to all countries, and relevant to any number of situations. I propose the following five scales:

0	1	2	3	4	5	6	7	8	9	10

Equality   Hierarchy

Direct   Indirect

Individual   Group

Task   Relationship

Risk   Caution

I did not invent the categories of equality, hierarchy, caution, risk, and so forth. I have chosen these terms for the sake of simplicity because I find they make more sense to people than some of the jargon others use. Nor are the concepts the terms represent mine. Each one of these five basic dimensions is widely written about in some way, just as there are multitudes of fitness books that include the basic concepts such as fats or carbohydrates or exercise in various combinations or with various approaches.

For a long time I have chosen to use four (and most recently five) dimensions in the hope of keeping things simple but still offering something meaningful. I find most people can keep track of four or five scales (but their eyes might glaze over with ten) and that these five dimensions offer a solid starting point for describing cultural differences. These five scales can help the reader understand his or her "cultural style" (then compare or contrast it with others') in much the same way the popular Myers-Briggs Type Indicator® helps people understand and then compare their personality style with others'.

It might be hard to believe that I've *never* been comfortable with two-part dichotomies, since I use them so much in this book. Philosophers and professors often like to spur their students or audiences into debate with questions like "Is teaching an art or a science?" or "Are people inherently good or evil?" or "What's more important, nature or nurture?"

Biologists have *needed* to classify, starting at the most basic level, deciding if something should be catalogued as a plant or as an animal, a vertebrate or an invertebrate, a species that gives birth to live young or lays eggs.

I wouldn't worry about it—they're probably just dolphins.

These basic distinctions are both useful and necessary for biology, but they are not the final word in understanding an animal and its behavior. At low levels of categorization, cats and dogs end up looking pretty much the same: they are both covered with fur, have four legs, give birth to live young, and so forth. But those who have cats and dogs as pets know how different they are from each other. Ever tried to teach your cat to sit, stay, heel, or fetch? Try dropping your dog and see if she consistently lands on her feet like cats do. No, don't! Try teaching her to stalk mice instead!

A dog trainer needs to understand the intricacies of how dogs think and behave and what motivates them. Knowing that dogs are "basically like cats, but somewhat different" does not qualify you for a job as head dog trainer. The analogy also applies to people, and I want you to keep this in mind as you consider the five scales below. You need to know both your own and the other person's cultural "species" pretty intimately. If she's an Egyptian, don't treat her like a Swiss!

The simple scales I present here, with their dichotomous approach, are a *starting* point. Simplicity is good when it's used as a starting point, not a final answer. Understanding culture is, and should be, a messy and complicated business (and an enjoyable one) the deeper you get, so be sure to not oversimplify it.

All that said (whew!), let's look at the five scales and what each means.

Equality versus Hierarchy

This first scale relates to a variety of issues which, like all five scales, may manifest at the individual level, at the organizational level, and at the level of national cultures. For example, some organizations are structures of people who are on essentially equal footing with their co-workers. Other organizations have more distinct roles about who is in charge and who is responsible for what. Looking down to the individual level, we will see that individuals within either organizational scenario prefer to interact in more egalitarian or more hierarchical ways. And looking more broadly to the societal level, we will see that some countries or regions may prefer equality-based or hierarchy-based approaches.

The cliché that there are exceptions to every rule really does apply here: in the most egalitarian society, it would not be appropriate for a low-ranking military clerk to say to the division commander, "Hey, Joe, c'mon into my office for a moment, would you." Military or governmental organizations will tend to be hierarchically oriented in any country, just as small companies in the creative industries might tend to be more egalitarian. And regardless of the country or organization, individuals will prove to be exceptions to the rule because they will have preferences that are counter to the norm.

That said, let's consider a case with issues relevant to this scale (these cases use fictitious names, of course).

Case 1—Equality/Heirarchy Scale

Mark, a recently arrived American manager in India, was complaining to his American associate, "I've been finding that I need to give much more detailed, specific instructions to these people than I would to Americans back home in order to get even the simplest things done. And unless such minute detail is provided, problems usually develop. These people don't seem to take the initiative to do anything other than what is clearly outlined in advance. I know they are smart....I've seen a lot of innovative work on their part...they have a lot of creative ideas, really. But they don't seem to want to share them with me. I feel that they just want me to tell them what to do and then leave them alone to do it. What am I doing wrong? What can I do to help them feel more comfortable with me?"

What do you think might explain the manager's frustrations in this case? Here are six possibilities:

1. The Indians Mark deals with respect his position as manager and expect him to tell them what to do.

2. Mark is experiencing cultural adjustment issues, and because of this he is easily irritated by even small things that seem to go wrong.

3. Indian workers are not very detail oriented, so the details must be provided to them.

4. The workers Mark is referring to are accustomed to a strong style of top-down leadership and do not usually presume to participate in decisions with their superiors.

5. Mark must have pushed the Indians too far already and they are not interested in working with him.

6. Indians are lazy and unless given detailed instructions, they won't perform.

Some of these answers are stereotypes. Answers 3 and 6 fit in this category and probably aren't helpful in making sense of the manager's confusion. To say someone is lazy is to use an all-too-common negative stereotype. And of course, it's an absurdly overreaching stereotype to suggest that all people from a particular culture might not be detail oriented.

Some of the answers use behaviors to explain what may have gone wrong. Answers 2 and 5 fall in this category. Becoming irritated at something going wrong or having pushed the Indians too far are possible interpretations of Mark's actions or behaviors; we don't know. While these may or may not be accurate descriptions of what happened, they certainly don't offer us a general principle to follow, because people's behaviors change in every situation.

It's true that behaviors are what we really see and must deal with. But the remaining answers, 1 and 4, give us insights into some general principles that could apply to a variety of situations our manager Mark may encounter when dealing with Indians (and, likely, other Easterners). These answers address the deeper-level phenomenon of focusing on either *equality* (where employees are granted the power to take initiative even if they don't have a position or title after their name) or *hierarchy* (where the manager is expected to take control and make the decisions).

Looking deeper than what is visible on the outside (above the waterline on the iceberg), looking beyond employee behaviors and considering the possible deeper meanings—these can teach us something useful that we can apply in a variety of situations or cultures.

The chart below contains a brief summary of some of the issues that relate to the equality versus hierarchy scale. Read through the descriptions and

Equality: Where employees are granted the power to take initiative even if they don't have a position or title after their name.

Hierarchy: Where the manager is expected to take control and make the decisions.

ask yourself which side you identify with the most. Where would you place your international customers, clients, partners, or counterparts? [†]

	0	1	2	3	4	5	6	7	8	9	10	
Equality ←												→ Hierarchy

A style that is based on *equality* means people prefer to

- be self-directed,
- have flexibility in the roles they play in a company or on a team,
- have the freedom to challenge the opinion of those in power,
- make exceptions, be flexible, and maybe bend the rules, and
- treat men and women in basically the same way.

A style that is based on *hierarchy* means people prefer to

- take direction from those above,
- have strong limitations about appropriate behavior for certain roles,
- respect and not challenge the opinions of those who are in power because of their status and their position,
- enforce regulations and guidelines, and
- expect men and women to behave differently and to be treated differently.

[†] To find your personal style on this scale and on the other four culture scales in this book, you might want to try the Peterson Cultural Style Indicator™ online. See the Appendix for further information on this tool.

Direct versus Indirect

This second culture scale relates to the way people communicate and interact with one another in face-to-face verbal and nonverbal communication and in written communication. This scale is a simple one to understand and an important one to know about.

You are certainly already aware that some people within your own culture communicate more directly than others. You probably know co-workers who don't mind getting "in your face" and challenging you on an issue and other co-workers who are more tactful. While personality differences certainly affect communication style, it's important to know that a culture as a whole can be said to be more or less direct. In many Asian cultures, for example, people recognize and practice the concepts of "face" and harmony in ways Westerners do not. Being direct and "getting all the issues out on the table" can be a good thing (according to the Western view), but the Asian approach of setting some conflicts aside for the sake of maintaining a harmonious work environment or respectful communication is equally legitimate. Knowing which conflicts to take on and how directly to deal with them based on particular situations and cultures you are dealing with is the key to this second scale.

Consider this case:

Case 2—Direct/Indirect Scale

>Several months after beginning sales efforts in Japan, Lisa, an American manager, was discussing her new job challenges with a friend. At first, she had been charmed by the Japanese, especially by the fact that they were so nice. But now she is wondering if they are perhaps too nice. "For example," Lisa said to her friend, "I can never get clear feedback from the Japanese people I supervise. If I ask for their help in solving a problem, they always start by saying, 'This is just a suggestion, but....' And if I ask for input during a meeting, they will very rarely make negative statements. Isn't the idea to get all the pros and cons out on the table so that we can discuss things objectively? I think this politeness is going a little too far! What's going on?"

To be very direct and "get all the pros and cons out on the table" is a Western (and most noticeably American) tendency. Asians usually approach problems or difficulties in a more subtle, indirect way.

From the earliest age, Americans are taught to "say what we mean and mean what we say." As children, we are taught to speak up in class, to look people in the eye to show we are honest, and to present our views clearly. We are taught to be strong and to disagree verbally and nonverbally when we need to. To people in many non-Western cultures, direct eye contact is not a good thing but rather conveys a threat or challenge, and it is more important to maintain a sense of harmony or balance than to deal directly with issues, especially issues where there may be conflict.

An Asian who can't do something you request may simply not respond,

Q: Yes means yes, right!?

or she may say, "It's difficult" or even "Yes" or "No problem." On several occasions I have had Chinese people smile and tell me, "No problem!" when what they probably meant was "No way! *Big* problem!" But they simply would not have been comfortable being direct with me. By failing to say "No" when that is what they meant, they were not lying; rather they may have felt it was best to be indirect in order to keep things harmonious, and after all, they knew things would work out. On the other

A: It depends.

hand, if an American thinks yes, he will say "Yes." If an American can't or won't do something, he will likely say "No" (and if it's a big problem, the American certainly won't take the Chinese approach of saying "No problem!"). Many people around the world often choose to take the approach of "telling the Americans what they want to hear" because they may feel that to be truly direct could lead to useless or counterproductive conflict.

I used a Japanese example in Case 2 above because there is a clear contrast to be seen between East and West when we consider the United States and Japan. In this case, the American manager, Lisa, was probably frustrated because she didn't understand the Japanese indirect communication style. These issues are also at play to different degrees in the Middle East, some parts of Europe, and South America.

Earlier in this section I suggested that it is important to not over-simplify and that we should consider the many interesting gray areas between the two opposite extremes of any given culture scale. I would now add that we should consider the interplay among the five culture scales. For example, a more complete explanation of Case 2 might involve ideas from both this second culture scale (direct versus indirect) and from the first culture scale (equality versus hierarchy). People who are more hierarchically focused may not want to confront those in a position of power, and that might also help explain the reluctance of the employees in Case 2 to offer their opinions.

I have presented only two of five culture scales and already we can begin to see an overlap of issues or some kind of connection between the two scales. As you think about applying the five culture scales to your own issues, I encourage you to pick and choose various concepts from the scales you feel best explain the situation. The five scales are intended as a simple starting point, but I again discourage oversimplification and I encourage you to look for overlapping ideas among the five scales. While I strive for a simple starting point in my descriptions of culture, I would also say that describing cultures is, and should be, a complex and intricate process!

Below is a basic outline of some main issues that relate to this second culture scale:

| 0 | 1 | 2 | 3 | 4 | 5 | 6 | 7 | 8 | 9 | 10 |

Direct ◄──────────────────────────────────► Indirect

A *direct* style means people prefer to
- be more direct in speaking and be less concerned about how something is said,
- openly confront issues or difficulties,
- communicate concerns straight-forwardly,
- engage in conflict when necessary,
- express views or opinions in a frank manner, and
- say things clearly, not leaving much open to interpretation.

An *indirect* style means people prefer to
- focus not just on what is said but on how it is said,
- discreetly avoid difficult or contentious issues,
- express concerns tactfully,
- avoid conflict if at all possible,
- express views or opinions diplomatically, and
- count on the listener to interpret meaning.

Again, read through the descriptions and ask yourself which side you identify with the most. Then try to judge where you would place the people from other countries whom you mix with professionally.

Individual versus Group Orientation

This third culture scale deals essentially with the degree of importance that people give to being part of a group, be it family, friendship, or work related. People in various societies place more or less importance on which groups they belong to and how strong their attachment is to those groups. This idea is sometimes referred to as "in-groups" versus "out-groups." Some tend to identify strongly with the same groups for their entire lives, and they don't transition very easily in and out of these groups; others have weaker group affiliations and can be more casual in joining or dropping out of groups. For example, people from group-oriented cultures might maintain lifelong affiliations with their high school or college peers. It may also take them quite some time to be counted as a member of a group, but once they are in, they're "in for life" (or at least for the long term). The loyalty of employees to the company (and vice versa) is high, so lifelong employment is common in group-oriented cultures. In contrast, people from individualistic cultures usually identify less strongly with work, friendship, or even family groups (instead defining themselves by who they are as individuals); they will transition more quickly and easily in and out of various groups in various phases of their lives, and workplace loyalty (on the part of the employee and employer) can be low, even negligible. Employees from individualistic cultures often leave a company for a better opportunity, even if it involves moving and layoffs are more common than lifelong employment.

I need to make a distinction here between individualism and individuality. I define the term *individualism* as "the promotion of one's own needs; putting oneself first." *Individuality*, on the other hand, suggests that "each person is unique and has some kind of different personal contribution to make." The reason I make this distinction is because in various programs I have conducted on French culture (and this applies to a variety of others too), the French will almost always rank themselves toward the "individual" side of this scale. Yet France certainly has a stronger group orientation than the United States does in some ways: socialized medicine (versus individually funded health insurance), nationally funded education (versus individual responsibility for college tuition), public mass transportation (versus the individualistic automobile), and so forth. Still, the French are correct in pointing out their individual focus; they do value the articulate expression of an individual's ideas and the uniqueness of each person. This apparent contrast can be reconciled by the distinction between individualism (which describes Americans well) versus individuality (which describes the French and many other Westerners).

Try this as an informal test of in-groups and out-groups: notice how you interact with total strangers while passing on the street. One of the ways you can tell whether a culture is individualistic or group focused is by paying attention to how strangers interact (or fail to interact) with you. Because Americans can have loosely defined in-groups, we can easily interact with just about anybody. Notice how Americans passing on the street can acknowledge total strangers with a nod of the head or a wave of the hand or even greet them verbally with "Hello," "Good morning," and so forth. (Of course this does not apply equally to businesspeople rushing to lunch in New York City or people out for an evening stroll in a small town in Kansas.) In contrast, people from group-oriented cultures tend not to greet or even acknowledge strangers on the street. Because the strangers are an out-group, it's not necessary to even say hello.

Case 3—Individual/Group Scale

Amy, a twenty-eight-year-old manager in a global freight company headquartered in the United States communicates via fax, phone, and e-mail almost daily with international colleagues. Amy describes her job as "putting out brushfires" and "finding creative solutions." She is a capable, motivated, and productive employee who is good at what she does. Like her colleagues, Amy is largely self-directed because her company, though it has 10,000 employees worldwide and two billion dollars in revenue, lacks some formal structures such as an HR department. It is part of the company culture that employees are expected to be creative problem solvers who can think clearly and quickly and take the necessary actions to get things done.

Amy's current task is to communicate, negotiate, and find solutions for various aspects of some new shipping procedures with her Venezuelan partners. She does this via telephone and frequent e-mail with her main Venezuelan contact, a man named Juan Carlos. Amy is somewhat frustrated because she feels she spends half her time waiting for answers, especially for the more complex questions or changes in procedure. But why are the Venezuelans so slow? This is a fast-moving business! She is beginning to wonder whether these Venezuelans are showing a version of the Mexican "mañana" attitude.

What do you think might best explain the situation?

1. A Venezuelan man doesn't respect a female colleague as much as he would a male colleague.

2. The Venezuelans may be stalling because they feel Americans are too pushy or too much in a hurry.

3. Juan Carlos is not expected to decide things on his own when his decisions could significantly affect the way his colleagues do their jobs.

4. Language barriers naturally result in delays. The Venezuelans are probably translating the various communications into Spanish before responding.

5. It's often a simple question of the Venezuelans not understanding the paperwork or knowing the shipping restrictions, so they have to do more research before responding.

6. The decision-making process may be slower for Venezuelans because there is more communication among team members.

The first answer is probably the strongest stereotype (and a very inaccurate one). The second answer is also a stereotype, and if you're an American, I'll let you be the judge of its accuracy. While it's certainly true that language barriers (answer 4) and paperwork (answer 5) often result in delays, answers 3 and 6 might guide us toward understanding some deeper ideas about how group and individual cultures work. Amy prides herself on the fact that she is often able to respond immediately to diverse situations. She has proven that she "knows her stuff," and she is used to acting on her own. These skills serve her well in her own system. In countries that are more group oriented than the United States, however, this kind of employee autonomy and individual initiative may not be valued as much as the ability to function well in a group or to follow orders from above. Answers 3 and 6 are in this vein. Juan Carlos may not be authorized to make decisions; or he may be expected to involve his colleagues in decisions that affect them. He has not been groomed to be the stand-alone go-getter in the same way his American equivalents might have been.

I offer the following models (A, B, and C below) as a way of illustrating different behaviors in individualistic versus group-focused cultures. These three illustrations show how people in different cultures may have different kinds of "walls" around themselves. Let's look at three groups in very broad terms:

North Americans (represented by diagram A) tend to be approachable and outgoing, with a rather thin "outer wall" surrounding them. They tend to move easily in and out of social groups, consider themselves quite friendly, and let new people past this thin outer wall quite easily. They also tend to be quite willing to relocate themselves and their families where career opportunities call, to other regions or even other countries where they have no ties at all.

Some Europeans and South Americans (diagram B) have a thicker outer wall. It takes more time before they let people past the thick outer wall in diagram B, that is, more time to develop close affiliations and accept someone into their group. But once someone is part of a group, he or she will tend to have lifelong relationships that will continue to develop over months and years. A higher salary or faster career track may not motivate people in group-focused cultures to relocate to another region or country if it would mean distance from long-established friends, family, neighbors, and community.

Many Asians (diagram C) have a very thin outer wall just outside of the thick, protective one. The model is like diagram B except for the thin outer wall, which represents the Asian emphasis on harmony, proper hosting, courtesy, protocol, and so forth in business and social relationships.

Diagram A can be a good model for describing individually focused cultures, and B and C can describe group-focused cultures. Of course,

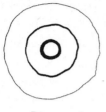

Diagram A

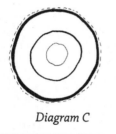

Diagram B

Diagram C

the above comments are prese[...] very general terms, lumping toge[...] all U.S. and Canadian Americans, al[...] Europeans and South Americans, and all Asians. Important cultural differences exist within these geographical areas, but the examples above are a first "big picture" look.

One American manager told me after a two-week house-hunting trip to Japan that he found the Japanese to be very friendly, warm people and that he was sure he would have no trouble fitting in during his two or three years there. How many walls had he breached? My guess would be just the thin outer dotted line of diagram C! Very likely the Japanese had indeed hosted him warmly but had barely, if at all, begun to consider him truly part of their group.

What typically happens in this kind of situation is that eventually the expatriates and their families begin to notice that they are not being invited over to homes or they are *somehow* not building friendships, good working relationships, or a support network in the same way they could if they had relocated within their own country.

In the workplace, people from individualistically oriented cultures can be frustrated at how slowly meaningful connections are built in the beginning when they work with people from group-focused cultures. And those from group-focused cultures sometimes perceive people from individualistic cultures as shallow or insincere because they seem to move so quickly to familiarity with others.

Beliefs about group or individual identity determine whether you will readily call someone a friend (Americans puzzle Europeans by referring to mere acquaintances as "a friend of mine"), the level of ŀy, decision-making style, relationship-building ŀyles, and other issues.

ŀllet-points summary of themes that can make up ŀle. As before, read through the descriptions and ŀide best describes you. Then try to judge where ŀ people from other countries whom you mix with professionally.

```
        0   1   2   3   4   5   6   7   8   9   10
```
Individual ◄─────────────────────────────────► **Group**

An *individual* style means people prefer to	A *group* style means people prefer to
• take individual initiative,	• act cooperatively and establish group goals,
• use personal guidelines in personal situations,	• standardize guidelines,
• focus on themselves,	• make loyalty to friends a high priority,
• judge people based on individual traits,	• determine their identity through group affiliation,
• make decisions individually,	• make decisions as a group,
• put individuals before the team,	• put the team or group before the individual,
• be nonconformists when necessary, and	• conform to social norms, and
• move in and out of groups as needed or desired.	• keep group membership for life.

Task versus Relationship

Common sense suggests that successful professional interaction with anyone (from any culture) requires some kind of focus on relationship building. People in every industry try to learn as much as possible about their clients, customers, and business partners. It naturally follows that the process of knowing these counterparts might become a bit trickier when they come from different cultures.

While this might seem like common sense, I find the common belief to be the opposite: many otherwise savvy American professionals have come right out and told me, "If you just be yourself, you'll get along fine with people from any culture" (which is sometimes followed by comments such as "Just talk about the weather or sports—especially soccer, which is called 'football' elsewhere"). The persistent myth is that after a bit of such introductory chitchat, the international counterpart will be ready to plunge into a business relationship. I suppose this is an attractive view; it would be nice if it were true. But it isn't, and that's quite apparent within the context of this fourth culture scale.

This scale relates to the process of putting relationship building and trust first and foremost in doing business versus placing business center stage—and if a personal relationship develops in the process, it's icing on the cake.

Americans are especially prone to ignoring the relationship side of the business equation because they see these as "soft skills" that can be left up to intuition. But when tossed into an international interaction, Americans are quickly forced to realize that the "soft skill" of business relationship building indeed has a very real impact on the "bottom line."

Predictably, people from relationship-focused cultures often feel pushed or rushed by task-focused Americans. It's typical for Americans to schedule a trip abroad lasting merely a few days or a week and hope to accomplish something meaningful with their overseas partners. This frustrates both sides. It frustrates the Americans, who had actually hoped to accomplish something concrete (like a price agreement or a signed contract) but who were not able to get down to business quickly enough, and it frustrates the international partners, who had hoped to begin building some kind of business relationship with the Americans but felt pushed and rushed toward making business decisions or commitments before they learned whether they could trust the American group.

Consider this case:

Case 4—Task/Relationship Scale

> *Shane is a chief engineer in an American company that will be partnering with a Singaporean company to manufacture a new model of digital camera in Singapore. Shane is sent on a five-day trip to Singapore, during which he plans to discuss a set of specific issues relating to both software (such as how the camera will be programmed to compensate for any bad pixels) and hardware (such as*

issues relating to the design of the circuit boards). Shane has two especially concrete goals for the trip: he has been instructed to have the Singaporeans help him choose a firm that could produce the first main circuit-board prototype, and he needs the Singaporeans to agree to some tentative production time goals.

The first day is lost because Shane arrives at 10:30 P.M. after more than twenty-four hours of travel. Jet lag isn't much of a problem for Shane the second day; he's full of energy. He is pleasantly surprised to find himself being treated like a king, with doors courteously opened for him and always being seated at the head of the table during meals and meetings. The third day he is exhausted, but he is taken on a tour of two circuit-board factories, as planned. Shane feels like the honored (though exhausted) guest at yet another dinner on the third night. He tries to talk business during that dinner, but without his daytime interpreter at the table next to him, it's tedious in spite of the high English proficiency of the Singaporeans.

Shane feels a large chunk of time is lost on the fourth day when he and some of the Singaporean team are taken to play golf at a country club owned by the brother of one of the Singaporean engineers. The fifth day he urgently needs to agree to some tentative production time goals. The Singaporeans seem to agree with anything he proposes but don't appear to want to make real decisions or commitments. With the prospect of being at the airport at 6:30 A.M. the next day, Shane is distraught when this fifth and last full business day is taken up by yet another grand restaurant lunch, where he is the "honored guest." His interpreter is present, but the meal takes two hours and it's not a practical setting for getting business done. In the end, Shane has still not solidified any production time goals and it seems (though he's not sure) that his Singaporean counterparts may have already chosen which firm will produce the circuit-board prototype, though he is not sure what the choice is based on or who approved it.

Several elements of this all-too-typical case relate to the task versus relationship scale. As the American task-focused approach would dictate, Shane wanted to move straight to business. He had been charged with accomplishing aggressive goals in a very short time. To do this, he had probably expected to communicate his proposals and requests concisely and quickly and to hear clear answers to them. Aware of the short time frame in which he needed to accomplish his goals, Shane probably did not want to enjoy leisurely meals or a golf game. The language barrier and the jet lag also worked against Shane's accomplishing his goals.

In contrast to this, the more relationship-focused Singaporeans probably wanted to get to know Shane and his company before jumping straight to business. They made every effort to welcome Shane and to host him well. Their goals may have been to establish at least a sense of familiarity with Shane, upon which could be built a sense of mutual trust and then eventually a business relationship. These things would likely be more important to people from a relationship-focused culture than agreeing to any production schedules.

This case has another element that illustrates what can happen in relationship-focused cultures: the selection of a circuit-board manufacturer had essentially been done before Shane even arrived because the Singaporeans already had a long-standing history of working with a manufacturing facility owned by a relative of one member of the Singaporean team. That established relationship was more important than finding a new firm that was up to the task of making the circuit boards.

Another way of understanding task versus relationship is to think of who we *are* versus what we *do*.

Several years ago I attended the wedding of an old college friend. At her wedding I met her father for the first time. He was a successful entrepreneur who had started several businesses and sold them at great profit. He also came from an old wealthy family of self-made high achievers.

As he walked around, meeting his daughter's college friends for the first time, he shook hands with each person and offered a sincere "Nice to meet you," then asked, *"What do you do?"*

This successful American businessman's way of first getting to know people was by asking what work they did. In fact, many Americans form their identity based on what they do.

The American handshake:
"Glad to meetcha! What do you do?"

What do people from relationship-oriented cultures talk about if they don't primarily discuss what they do? Any variety of things. Start by showing a genuine interest in your international counterparts and asking sincere questions about them. Your discussion might lead into larger themes such as art, history, and literature or more common themes such as music, current trends and popular issues, food, or leisure activities (recall the table on page 25). You might not be an expert on the topics you discuss, but rather than trying to hide your ignorance, show a genuine curiosity! Of course you shouldn't go so far as to interrogate the person, but usually people are glad to talk about their own country and culture—as long as you ask informed questions. The section in Part 6 entitled "Target Country Knowledge" offers more detailed recommendations for how you can study other cultures' history, economics, and social and ethnic issues. One very good way to explore those issues can be through discussions with natives from the culture in question.

Now, the question of what to talk about besides work can be a little misleading, because usually the first thing businesspeople from anywhere need to know may in fact be what their counterparts do. That's to be expected. But even if it is the first thing they want to know, it's not necessarily the primary thing. There are any number of ways to get to know a person better and any number of topics to discuss in doing so.

Here's an exercise: try introducing yourself to someone without mentioning your job or your profession. Just talk about who you are. You might find you have surprisingly little to say! How would you approach this? Would you define yourself by your family? (I have noticed that many Asians introduce themselves by telling about their families—"I am from a family of five. I live with my two sisters, my parents, and my grandparents"—in addition to telling about what their job role is.) Or would you define yourself by where you live? By what you like? By what you think is important? By what you have learned recently? Would those seem like awkward things to talk about? If so, then how indeed would you explain who you are without referring to what you do? In the United States we are so "doing" oriented that it may be hard to define ourselves in any other way!

People in "being"-oriented countries often rank leisure time higher than work time in their priorities (work to live, not live to work). For example, in Sweden workers only rarely stay in the office past 5:00 P.M., and the minimum vacation is five weeks. The French enjoy those same four or five weeks of vacation, and (in order to reduce unemployment) the French government mandated, starting around 2000, that various types of businesses must begin to reduce their workweek from thirty-eight to thirty-five hours.

The French or the Swedes may tell you, however, "Bah—this is changing! Now more and more of us are working long hours just like Americans...especially those who work for the bigger international companies." I'll accept that. There's certainly a difference between "traditional Sweden" and what we might call, perhaps unfortunately, "Americanized corporate Sweden," so my general statement will not apply to all companies or all workers. It's interesting, though, that when people say they are working long hours, they equate that with becoming "Americanized." We will be wrong some of the time when making general statements like this, but at least we have an idea that many nations don't focus on work to the extent that the United States does.

Now, are the Swedes and the French (and many others) lazy workers? Of course not! In fact both Sweden and France are advanced, high-tech coun-

> **Is your style "business before pleasure" or "pleasure before business"?**

tries that simply have different business and cultural values than the United States does. There is less emphasis on work (what you do) and more emphasis on the quality of life (who you are outside work). In the U.S. we say "business before pleasure" and in much of the rest of the world it's "pleasure before business" and "trust before business."

Following is a summary of issues that relate to this fourth culture scale. As you did for the first three scales, ask yourself which descriptions you relate to the most and try to place your international partners on this scale, too.

```
     0  1  2  3  4  5  6  7  8  9  10
Task ◄─────────────────────────────► Relationship
```

A *task* style means people prefer to	A *relationship* style means people prefer to
• define people based on what they do,	• define people based on who they are,
• move straight to business—relationships come later,	• establish comfortable relationships and a sense of mutual trust before getting down to business,
• keep most relationships with co-workers impersonal,	• have personal relationships with co-workers,
• sacrifice leisure time and time with family in favor of work,	• sacrifice work in favor of leisure time and time with family,
• get to know co-workers and colleagues quickly but usually superficially,	• get to know co-workers and colleagues slowly and in depth,
• use largely impersonal selection criteria in hiring (such as résumés or test scores), and	• use largely personal selection criteria (such as family connections) when hiring, and
• allow work to overlap with personal time.	• not allow work to impinge on personal life.

Risk versus Caution

Americans make macho statements about risk and change: "We eat change for breakfast!" boasts an American printing company. Numerous American consulting firms claim to help their clients "thrive on risk." You could correctly say that no professional around the world can escape dealing in some way with the risks, changes, uncertainties, newness, and ambiguities of an ever-evolving world. But the United States seems to pride itself on its ability to embrace change and face risk.

The United States has indeed been successful in various ways specifically because Americans embrace change and welcome risk. For example, consider this crazy concept: imagine gathering up a bunch of wood, fabric, wires, bolts, and other odd parts and a used engine and somehow assembling it all into your own flying machine that can physically pick you up and transport you through the air. Certainly a risky proposition! And it was indeed Americans who made the first air-plane flight. Americans also harnessed electricity and put it to a variety of uses from the light bulb to the microwave oven. In the very recent past, Americans have invented or been the first to capitalize on a wide range of other items from computers to televisions to automobiles to moving pictures to refrigerators to washing machines (and the list goes on). Americans are certainly not the only inventors on earth (far from it!), but I believe Americans are prolific inventors in large part because of their comfort with risk.

Consider how the element of time might affect peoples' prefer-ences for risk or caution: How long has your culture been around? Five thousand years or two hundred years? New countries that have only been in existence for a few hundred years (i.e., Australia, Canada, New Zealand, the United States) have had to take risks to build themselves from nothing. Striking off across an ocean for a relatively unknown geographical destination and a new world involves risk. No wonder not many years later these same people are off exploring the moon!

In contrast to this willingness to plunge into new frontiers and take risks, older, more established cultures prefer caution and know they can well afford to take their time. Cultures that are caution oriented can be good at carefully planning and then methodically and scientifi-cally proceeding in their ventures (and this may often mean proceeding relatively slowly). Such deliberate caution and patience is a wonderful asset that can produce results far superior to what can be achieved by plunging in quickly and taking risks.

Precision manufacturing and engineering are naturally done best by caution-oriented cultures such as Germany or Japan. Americans may have invented quite a few things, but others can legitimately claim to be better at producing the items with top quality standards. The fam-ily of a German friend of mine has operated a vineyard for about three hundred years. His family chuckles when the relatively brand-new vine-yards in California claim to know what they are doing! How could the California vintners possibly interact

> **Americans are good at sketching out the orig-inal rough draft on a blank canvas; the Ger-mans and Japanese are the masters at paint-ing in the beautifully finished details.**

as peers with the Germans? The Californians might have good insights into wine making based on new technologies or science, but it would take some convincing for the Germans to take the Californians' work seriously or to trust that they know what they are doing.

This of course applies to many fields outside wine making. In many kinds of business partnership, Americans typically feel ready and confident to launch into new ventures; where there is no precedent, a new one can be forged. Many others around the world often want to proceed more slowly and cautiously because their businesses (and cultures) have often existed for a longer time and have a greater historical perspective to consider.

Case 5—Risk/Caution Scale

Michael, an American director in charge of developing new markets in Eastern Europe in the home improvement and building sector, is frustrated with the slow progress and seemingly unnecessary delays he encounters. "These people want to see every last detail worked out before they can even think of moving forward," he complains. "Every little change in procedure needs to be documented. Just when I think we have something squared away, some new hassle pops up or some obscure building code or regulation surfaces. Sometimes it's an administrative issue; sometimes it's a request for further information when I thought we had everything out on the table. I can never predict what the delay will be. Introducing this product into the region will help these people—it will improve their lives and they recognize that, so why don't they make it easier to bring something to market? Can't these people handle anything new?"

This kind of frustration is typical for Americans who try to enter a variety of new markets around the world. In addition to the preference for caution and careful planning described above, it's important to realize the simple fact that people have been able to make do quite well without American products or services for the last several thousand years. People who have survived perfectly well without American products, institutions, technologies, hospitals, and hotels for generations may not desire them as urgently as the Americans feel they must be built, introduced, or sold.

Below are bullet points showing elements on the opposite ends of the risk-caution culture scale. As before, determine which descriptions fit you—and your international colleagues—best.

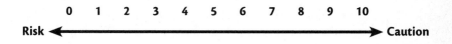

```
      0   1   2   3   4   5   6   7   8   9   10
Risk  ◄───────────────────────────────────►  Caution
```

A *risk* style means people prefer to
- make decisions quickly with little information,
- focus on present and future,
- be less cautious—in a "ready, fire, aim" way,
- change quickly without fear of risks,
- try new and innovative ways of doing things,
- use new methods for solving problems,
- have fewer rules, regulations, guidelines, and directions, and
- be comfortable changing plans at the last minute.

A *caution* style means people prefer to
- collect considerable information before making a decision,
- focus on the past,
- be more cautious—in a "ready, aim, aim, fire" way,
- change slowly and avoid risks,
- want more rules, regulations, guidelines, and directions,
- refer to past precedents of what works and what doesn't,
- stick to proven methods for solving problems, and
- not change plans at the last minute.

So is a risk orientation desirable or inherently good? And is a caution focus a liability? A Chinese friend complained to me about his own culture's aversion to risk and change in this way: "What have the Chinese invented since gunpowder and paper thousands of years ago?" But here I must quickly point out that a risk orientation is not inherently positive, and the opposite, a caution orientation, is certainly not inherently negative.

The answer therefore, as with every one of these five culture scales, is that neither extreme (risk or caution) is inherently superior to the other, but each style has advantages and disadvantages that can come into play in various situations. It is up to you, the internationally focused professional, to tap into the positive elements of the cultural preferences of those you interact with.

Overlapping the Five Scales

I've included one brief case in the discussion of each of the five culture scales because case studies usually make one isolated point concisely. But as I suggested before, themes from all five scales can overlap in various ways and situations.

A pair of e-mails I actually received from two prospective business partners illustrates how several elements of the five culture scales can be at play simultaneously. The basic background information is that one writer was Japanese and the other was Dutch. Each writer had the same purpose: seeking a business partnership with me. Each person had exchanged e-mails with me just once before; these were their second e-mails to me. The Japanese e-mail was as follows:

> *Dear Dr. Peterson,*
>
> *Hello. This is (first and last name) again. I reviewed your Website over the weekend, and I came up with many questions for you. Yes. I am quite excited about this opportunity already.*
>
> *First of all, I would like to tell you that I am very impressed with your work. I am sure that it would be a wonderful opportunity for me and I would learn so much if I can work with you.*
>
> *Well, here come my questions:*
>
> 1. *How do you usually market your service? Do you mainly rely on your Website or do you depend more on personal connections? Or do you actually go out and sell yourself? Or phone? Flyer? Do you have a sales team?*
> *If I were to work with you, I think I would be able to utilize many of the devices mentioned above. I have some personal connections in the area, since I have been living in this area for ten years, and I also established many connections with Japanese businessmen in the area through my research project. Also, I would be able to go out and sell to any potential clients.*
> *However, my biggest concern is whether or not some organizations would be willing to have a consultant*

come all the way from Minneapolis. Sorry if I offended you somehow. Since I am quite new to this field and I have only worked with some consultants who are also in this area, I am not so familiar with the system yet. I am sure that it all depends on how I or we sell your service, though. Do you often get to do consulting/ training jobs outside your area? How about the San Francisco Bay area?

2. *Do you usually use any sort of catalogue or brochure for marketing purposes? If you do, I would love to take a look. For that matter, I would love to take a look on your products if I were to work with you.*

3. *Do you keep any feedback or comments from your clients who have used your service before? I thought that such comments would be a very good tool for me to use for marketing your service.*

4. *If I were to work with you, would it be possible for me to have some sort of training to learn more about your organization as well as your work? It does not have to be an actual meeting. However, it would be great if I could learn more about your organization to be more comfortable and confident about what I would be doing.*

5. *This is still a very tentative thought. However, I am thinking of relocating to New York City some time soon. I am not sure yet. Would it be a problem for you to work with me if I move to New York?*

These were the questions I came up with while I was reviewing your Website. I am sure that I will have some more, or you will have some questions for me, for that matter. If any of the questions above offended you or sounded silly, please forgive me. It is just because of my unfamiliarity to the business. I am totally enthusiastic about gaining such experiences and knowledge on this business. I hope I didn't represent myself incapable to work with, though.

I look forward to hearing from you very soon.

Sincerely, (first and last name)

We can see that the Japanese writer tends to fall somewhere toward these areas of the culture scales:

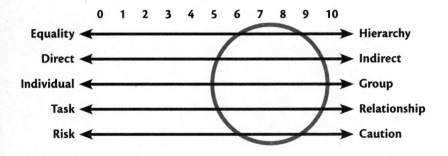

The Japanese writer showed an orientation toward hierarchy by calling me "Dr. Peterson." He was indirect in that he used tact with sensitive issues, complimented my work, and wrote with a tone of courtesy, humility, and diplomacy. His group orientation might be seen in his references to my sales team, his comments about personal connections and others he has worked with, and his questions about my organization. Overall the letter indicates a preference for developing a business relationship instead of "getting right down to the task at hand," and the many detailed questions may very well be indicative of a caution orientation.

In contrast, below is the e-mail I received from a Dutchman who had the same objectives as the Japanese writer. Here is the entire text of the Dutch writer:

> *Thanks for your quick turnaround—you're a man of ACTION! And I love your positive response. It so happened that I am working on a Business Home Page right NOW. The timeline is rather short. By FAX I've sent you the general lay-out. I am still groping but have been proactive in getting the Page established. I wish you would consider making me the West Coast Rep for your firm so that I can legally establish a hyperlink to your site on my Page. Give me commission for any business I direct your way!*

The Dutch writer probably falls somewhere toward the opposite ends of the five culture scales from the Japanese writer.

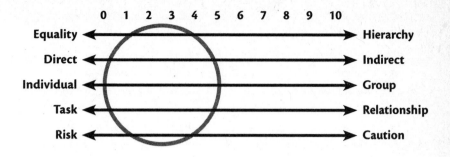

The Dutch writer shows an equality preference with his informal tone and the lack of title in addressing me. The Dutch writer clearly sees me as more of an equal without a hint of deference or formality. Unlike the Japanese writer, the Dutch writer does not include courtesies, introductions, or compliments; instead he directly proposes a business partnership and suggests I pay him commission. He is approaching me as an individual businessman without referring to my company, my team, or anyone he may be associated with. The entire Dutch letter is fewer than one hundred words because it has no opening or closing and gets straight to the task of discussing how we will do business. And the Dutchman's comfort with risk is evident when he explicitly writes that he wants to proceed and admits that he is "groping."

The e-mail is written in one paragraph as if the author were just tossing a few thoughts out. And all this took about as many words as the Japanese writer took to *introduce* his e-mail.

Of course, not every Japanese or Dutch person would write like these two did. But when we see examples of communication and interaction styles such as these letters illustrate, we can use the five culture scales to make sense of the differences and in turn decide how to respond in a culturally appropriate way.

Were the letters "culturally appropriate" for the situation at hand? Had they been writing to one another, it's easy to imagine that the Japanese person might have been offended by the Dutch writer's aggressive, no-holds-barred style and that the Dutch correspondent might have been impatient with the Japanese writer's wordiness and "obsequious" manner. But they were writing to me, and I happened to be quite comfortable with either style (because of the international exposure I'm fortunate to have had). Their letters were effective for what they hoped to accomplish, and that's probably the best way of answering that, yes, they were culturally appropriate.

In responding to the letters, I modified *my* style to fit theirs. I sent the Japanese person a longer e-mail with more courtesies of introduction and closing. My e-mail to the Dutchman was more informal, and so forth. But I don't try to "become Japanese" (or Dutch, or anything else) and write or communicate as a Japanese person when I am interacting with the Japanese. I am aware of ways in which I might benefit by modifying my style, but I am still an American, and because they are aware that they are dealing with an American, they will not expect me to become Japanese. In fact, I might look absurd if I were "too Japanese" in my response, because I could never be truly Japanese—I could never get it quite right.

Another thing to consider is that these people wanted my cooperation and positive response more than I may have wanted something from them. It's said that you can buy anything in your own language, but you need to sell things in "their" language. The same can be said about culture: to the extent that you desperately need the business, you must modify your style. If the roles had been reversed and I had been seeking the partnership with the Japanese or Dutch writers, I would have paid more attention to modifying my own style to fit their culture.

Professionals need a communication strategy that is appropriate for each task and each specific culture they do business with. This is true for writing simple letters and e-mails, but it is also important for bigger issues such as designing marketing pieces, selling product, dealing with complaints, making decisions, building workplace and social relationships, and managing people. Communicating appropriately with your international business partners certainly should not be left to intuition!

Every Culture Ranks Somewhere

As I wrote earlier, I believe that the United States is successful because of certain traits of American culture: the sense of equality, very direct style, individuality, focus on the task at hand, and willingness to take risks have served Americans well in various ways. The U.S. ranks somewhere toward the left extreme of the five culture scales, as illustrated in Figure A.

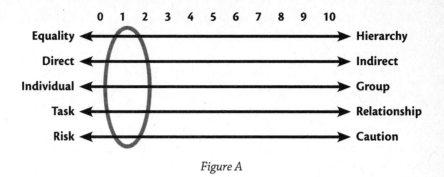

Figure A

Lest we develop inflated egos, though, I will quickly point out again that many other nations are also very successful and function smoothly precisely because of their cultural traits, many of which may be polar opposites of those of U.S. culture. Speaking in very general terms (yes, I'm grossly oversimplifying and exaggerating here), I will say that much of the rest of the world falls somewhere to the right of the United States, at various points on the five scales, as shown in Figure B.

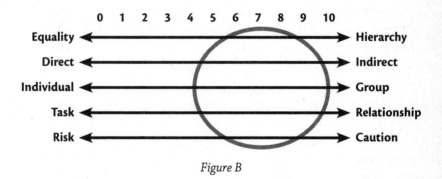

Figure B

This is admittedly extremely simplistic, but for our purposes, it is clearly a useful generalization if not an accurate final answer for every single country, company, or situation. The reason I make this simple contrast between the United States and much of the "rest of the world" is to encourage American professionals *not* to fall prey to the myth that "if you just be yourself, you'll get along fine with people from any culture." Americans would do well to prepare for cultural differences.

Those who argue "the whole world is becoming Americanized" may be partially right. Perhaps the circle in Figure B is shifting to the left in some ways. As American-style business spreads, people are adapting to a greater task orientation. They are learning to be more comfortable with risk, a direct style, informality, equality, and a more individual-istic lifestyle and career orientation as more of these choices become familiar and available.

At the same time, the circle in Figure A may be widening and shifting to the right. Americans are trying more teamwork principles (a group trait); learning to build relationships instead of jumping straight to the business task at hand; focusing on building and maintaining harmony with international colleagues (indirect style); remembering when to use last names and titles such as "Mr." or "Mrs." or "Doctor" (hierarchy) where appropriate with their international colleagues; being patient; and providing the proper information and reassurances to caution-ori-ented business partners; and so forth.

I don't find it useful to minimize cultural differences. Nor do I find it useful to exaggerate them. The world may be drifting toward similar-ity in some ways, but it is certainly maintaining distinctness in other ways. I don't find it realistic to talk about a "world culture," and I am horrified at the idea of cultural homogenization because I'm fascinated by cultural differences. So I recommend that internationally focused professionals expect, prepare for, and embrace cultural differences. Then it's possible to be pleasantly surprised when encountering cul-tural similarities. This is far better than expecting only similarities and being shocked by unanticipated differences.[‡]

[‡] For up-to-date rankings of over sixty specific countries on these five culture scales, see the Appendix for information on the Across Cultures online tools.

Part 2

The Importance of Culture in Daily Work and Life

Imagine yourself standing in the middle of an antique shop. Do you picture yourself surrounded by "junk" or by "treasures"? If you know something about antiques—their period, their function, or their history—then you see treasure in antique shops. If you don't know about these things, you may just see junk.

Looking at cultures can be similar. Some people see frustration (junk); others see fascination (treasures). Just as some of us can dismiss an entire antique shop with a wave of our hand, at some levels many of us dismiss other cultures because we judge them with an uninformed gaze.

We can be especially unobservant with cultures that seem to be similar. Some people think, "American, British, Canadian—what's the difference!? We all speak the same language, right?"

True, given the common language, it may seem as if it would be easier for the British, Americans, Australians, and Canadians to adjust to one another's cultures than it is for them to adjust to Asian, African, or Middle Eastern cultures. But even among these similar cultures, differences definitely exist and because of the expectation of familiarity, may pose more problems than you anticipate.

It makes sense that any office, team, or organization with a rich mix of cultural perspectives would be likely to excel, but the members' cross-cultural differences can also be barriers to successful performance. Internationally mixed organizations that are truly committed to success recognize that cultural differences, no matter how small they seem at first glance, are important to understand and to bridge.

Even when English is the first language of everyone in an internationally mixed organization, deeper differences can create invisible and very real challenges. For example, cultural and historical differences can result in different views on risk taking, planning preferences, styles of communication, levels of comfort with change, ways of dealing with conflict, degrees of formality, and other factors.

> **Even if everyone at the table speaks English, cultural differences can create powerful barriers to understanding.**

Here's an example one of my clients encountered. It appears that the job title of "engineer" may be more highly respected in England than it is in the United States. When a group of workers from England came to the U.S. on business, the Americans welcomed them and hosted them warmly, but they didn't give the engineers in the visiting group any special treatment to distinguish them from the rest of the group. The Americans didn't think it necessary, or probably even appropriate. The engineers in the group, however, were upset that they weren't singled out for special treatment, such as upgraded hotel rooms.

This might seem like a small slight, and it was in the beginning. But it is exactly the kind of thing that can start your business relationship off on a sour note. Wouldn't you rather have your international colleagues delighted with you? If the engineers are sitting in meetings, nursing their resentments over a perceived slight, you will have lost their support. Later on, they may not work as hard to meet deadlines, you may find projects delayed, and if more unintended insults continue to leave them disgruntled, you may ultimately lose sales.

Business flops usually don't happen suddenly because of surface-level gaffes such as improper handshakes, language flubs, or inappropriate attire at a meeting. Instead, international colleagues tend to become confused, frustrated, and irritated over time by the more subtle, invisible, usually unconscious cultural elements such as those the English engineers felt. These invisible elements come from something that could be called our deeper cultural programming. In the engineers' case it was the importance of hierarchy and status.

Cultural differences not only affect the way you do business internationally, they should also influence ways in which you operate with people inside your organization. The above comments relating to internationally or ethnically mixed workplaces relate also to domestic organizations with internationally or ethnically mixed clients, customers, or partners. Whether you're a hospital administrator, an auto manufacturer, or a university professor, having clients, patients, partners, students, or customers from multiple cultural backgrounds means multiple opportunities and multiple challenges. Providing products or services to people of diverse cultural backgrounds necessitates different strategies in marketing, sales, customer service, retention, recruitment, and so forth.

There are many aspects to and many ways of working together, and no matter what your business is, the influences of culture are inescapable today. I suggest that professionals do more than become minimally competent in understanding other cultures; they should become experts who are fascinated by the potential that differences offer (just as some are fascinated by antiques!). Substantial cultural differences do exist and definitely play a role in work and life with people from other cultures.

Cultural Programming

Just like computers, we are all programmed. Computers must use software to run, and humans have a "cultural programming" they can't operate without but that operates largely outside of awareness.

How important is our cultural programming?

Macintosh or Windows operating systems look similar at first glance. Both have monitors you look at, with a "desktop" holding a few icons. Both use a mouse

Put a Macintosh program in a Windows machine; put an American in Singapore.

and keyboard for input devices. Both have cords and wires coming out the back of a plastic central box that is the core of the computer. Both use printers. Both accomplish the same tasks. You could argue that the two systems are basically the same, with the same "look and feel."

In some ways, Mac and Windows systems can communicate well enough with each other, too. When I send e-mails from my Mac,

I don't have to be concerned about whether the recipients have Mac or Windows computers. They can use whatever system they want to open the e-mail at their end.

But try putting a Mac program into a Windows computer and you'll get an error message, because at the *programming level* the operating systems are significantly different.

This analogy applies to humans. A lot of participants in my cross-cultural programs seem to think that people all around the world are basically the same, and at first glance we do indeed seem similar. For example, people basically look the same (we are all human), have the same concerns (health, safety, food, shelter, etc.), and experience the same emotions (love, anger, fear, hatred, etc.). And, like computers, we are usually able to communicate, at least on the surface, across cultures. We send letters, faxes, and e-mails; we talk on the phone and sometimes communicate face to face.

But at a deeper level, people around the world do have significantly different cultural programming, just like computers do at the operating system level. Try to run an American-style business meeting (Americans will want to get straight to business, use people's first names as though they've been friends for years, dress and speak informally, move quickly, take risks, etc.) with European partners (some Europeans may want to get to know one another a bit

> Ironically, the Americans who think "We're all one world" and "People are basically the same everywhere" can get very territorial regarding their city, region, state, or country. They see supposedly huge differences right under their noses, but they can't quite see the even greater differences around the world.

before talking "money," perhaps feel more comfortable using titles and last names or at least more polite ways of addressing one another, dress stylishly, move cautiously to avoid risks, even be given some historical grounding) and you'll see that not everyone has the same "operating system."

There are differences within cities, where each neighborhood can have its own feel, and growing up on the "other side of the tracks" within a city can mean growing up in a totally different world.

If this is true, it *must* follow that daily life in Paris is probably *not exactly* like daily life in Calcutta. A resident of Calcutta is culturally programmed quite differently from a Parisian. At the surface level, it's easy to see: East Indians and the French dress differently because they live in areas of different weather patterns; they eat different food, use different transportation, enjoy different leisure activities, and so forth.

Deeper down, they may define family or marriage differently, may have divergent religious beliefs, and may not share similar knowledge and opinions on a variety of topics.

Deeper still, they may have different core values: friendship, convictions that are very strongly held and may not change as long as they live (e.g., humility, face, self-reliance), and so forth. At even deeper cultural programming levels, they probably have what amounts to quite different worldviews. They may view time as abundant or scarce or assume that a god is in charge of their fate or that they determine their own destiny.

There can be no doubt that various world regions do indeed have important differences in cultural programming. It's possible to categorize these into a "scale of differences."

The Scale of Differences

The "scale of differences" is a basic tool for describing the extent to which other cultures differ from our own.

In many ways, especially at the surface level, Canada and the United States are indeed quite similar. After all, Americans don't come back from a trip to Canada saying, *"Oh my god! Canada totally blew my mind! The people, the life, everything is so different there!"*

If an American places his or her home country at zero on a scale of differences going from 0 to 10, a Canadian is probably only different enough to register as a 1 or 1.5.

Canadians are somewhat different from Americans after all. Most visible are the facts that Canada is a bilingual country, it is much less densely populated, Canadians are fans of different sports, and so on. Going deeper, Canada has been formed by its own history, Canadians view and treat politicians differently, they have unique Canadian foreign policies, they play their own role in the world economy, and so

Canada totally blew Mike's mind!

forth. Deeper still, it could be said that Canadians are not as intensely individualistic as Americans and they have a variety of attitudes and values that are not identical to those of Americans. These attitude and value differences manifest in a number of ways: Canadians are less militaristic than Americans, viewing themselves as peacemakers and diplomats rather than the world's police. Canadians consider themselves moderate compared with the United States, which is seen as a land of "extremes" (ranging from antiabortionists to prochoice advocates; from war hawks to peace activists; from the super-rich to the chronically homeless). Canadians sacrifice some things to gain others; they have much tighter firearms control than Americans and safer streets. Free national health care means higher taxes for Canadians, but it may contribute to Canadians' higher life expectancy. The two countries differ in their immigration policies; some Canadians criticize the U.S. as being a melting pot where cultural identity is lost while they view Canada as a tapestry where the contribution of cultural differences is valued. Treatment of criminals is another area where Canadians and Americans have very different attitudes and systems. As you might guess, in some ways French Canadians present an even stronger contrast with Americans than do English-speaking Canadians.

Following is a scale for describing the levels of difference for places around the world. This is from a U.S. perspective. Obviously, the scale would need to be turned upside down or scrambled if you are from a different nation.

So, even though Americans don't usually come back from Canada and report, "Whoa! Canada totally blew my mind!" sometimes Americans *do* say this after they return from Nigeria or India. Seeing a dead body float down the Ganges (a form of burial) makes you stop and think. It's not the kind of thing you see every day in the United

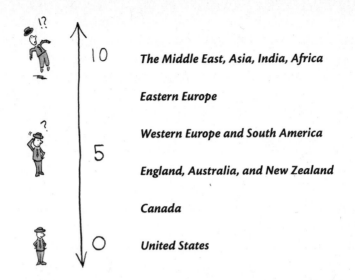

10   *The Middle East, Asia, India, Africa*

Eastern Europe

Western Europe and South America

5   *England, Australia, and New Zealand*

Canada

0   *United States*

States. Many Africans are animists; they believe that everything has a spirit—the tree, the antelope, the mountain. Although they may be Muslim or Christian, underneath they may still hold to at least some animistic beliefs and even practices. Does that strike you as strange? Yet some of the things that make perfect sense to Westerners are certainly seen as strange by others.

For example, isn't it ironic that Americans say they value freedom but accept so many limitations to their smaller freedoms? Strangely enough, in many places bars must close at 1:00 A.M. or risk losing their liquor licenses, and in many places alcohol cannot be sold in grocery stores or convenience stores. People in the United States can no longer smoke wherever they wish as people can in other countries. In many other countries, bars and restaurants close when the clientele is finished eating and drinking, no matter what time it is. In still other places, even a little child can buy wine in a grocery store (for the family), and people are not roped off into "smoking" or "no smoking" sections of restaurants. Non-Americans are often amazed at low U.S. speed limits and can't believe that an American driver can receive a ticket for going 35 or 36 mph in a 30-mph zone. And Americans can actually be ticketed for jaywalking! Elsewhere, people are expected to be responsible for themselves and accordingly are allowed more control over their own driving behavior and certainly the way they cross the street. These several examples of ways in which Americans allow themselves to be controlled can seem very strange to others. Americans may not have all the freedoms they believe they have.

Many kinds of thinking from abroad can be quite foreign to most Westerners. For example, most Westerners wouldn't seriously worry about whether their mate was born in a compatible calendar year, but the Chinese can take this seriously. The Chinese calendar follows a twelve-year cycle, and each year is associated with an animal. Some animal combinations are considered compatible and others are not. My Chinese friends can quickly identify what animal someone is according to his or her birth year. But whether a rabbit is compatible with a tiger is simply *not* something Americans pause to think about when considering a relationship.

When Canadians pick me up at the airport and meet me for the first time, they don't ask within the first few minutes, "Are you married? Do you have children? Do you have a girlfriend? Is she pretty? What year was she born?" The Chinese have asked me these very same questions within minutes of meeting me.

When I got together with some French friends I hadn't seen for more than a decade, they told me, "Oh! You've really fattened up and you look much older!" (Yes, I was nineteen and a skinny college student the last time I saw them.) For these people, calling someone "fat" is not a personal insult in the same way it can be for Americans.

Some might argue that these are just different ways of making conversation. But I maintain that the questions we ask, the conversations we have, the topics we consider appropriate, and the way we approach those topics all represent a deeper cultural programming. When the cultural programming between businesspeople from two sides is different enough,

> **Americans used to be able to do things abroad "the American way." Now, more choices for international partners means Americans need to make themselves culturally compatible or they will lose to someone else.**

they may ultimately choose to not do business with one another (or not be able to do business together).

Bottom-Line Business Choices

Question: Imagine you are considering doing business with one of two people, and imagine that both potential partners stack up about equally. That is, no matter which person you chose, you'd see about the same profits, the same benefits, the same share of the market. If the business opportunity is the same no matter whom you choose, how will you make your choice? All things being equal, what will the deciding factor be?

Answer: When I ask this question in my cross-cultural programs, participants from both East and West usually give one of two answers. They say without hesitation they'd choose the person they *trust* or the person they *like*.

Whether we trust and like people or mistrust and dislike them can have everything to do with similar or different cultural styles. The farther apart someone is from you on the scale of differences, the less likely you are to relate easily to that person. Sometimes the differences are simple ones, such as shaking hands with everyone in the room upon entering and leaving. Sometimes the differences are deeper ones, such as the fact that Americans like to take risks and push for quick action. This will instill mistrust in Saudis, who prefer the opposite. Japanese who remain calm, controlled, and poised will not make a positive impression on Brazilians, who express themselves with emotion and passion (and hand gestures that are not limited to the zone between the shoulders and waist!). The German preference for formality will seem stuffy, maybe even pretentious to Australians, who prefer to be informal.

There are multitudes of culture combinations that will usually make people feel ill at ease and many ways of perceiving others as "strange" (and **Do you naturally seek out awkward situations?** many ways for others to perceive us similarly). No one is to blame for this. But when people from two cultures get together, they often simply don't "click" because of cultural style differences. And when we don't click with someone, we tend to not like that person and to avoid them—and we certainly wouldn't trust him or her.

Now consider the opposite: think of a time when you've found it refreshing to meet someone similar to yourself. If you've been overseas for a long time, you know how reassuring it can be to meet someone from your home country, to finally hear your own language spoken by a native speaker, and to talk with someone in your own style. The simple truth is that most people do not seek out the uncomfortable, the different, or the awkward. If we feel awkward with people from other cultures (and if they feel awkward with us) and if we fail to click with them, they may not want to do business with us.

> Just because your cultural style makes you fantastically successful at home, it is not guaranteed to charm your international customers, clients, or partners. In fact, you can almost count on the opposite being true.

Choosing a business partner is similar; we select business partners we are comfortable with and trust. If we don't learn to overcome cultural differences enough to trust one another, we may lose business opportunities because a potential business partner's cultural style "rubs us the wrong way"—or vice versa.

Whether we trust or distrust someone, whether we like or dislike that person can be based, as I've said above, on intangible feelings. In addition to these "intangibles," there are some very tangible reasons why awareness of other cultures is important to our daily work and lives, and I will discuss those next.

Areas of Widespread Change

"It's a small world, and we have to think globally in order to be successful." Today, statements such as this are commonly tossed around and they do indeed reflect common sense. Maybe it will help our understanding to illustrate a few reasons why our world is shrinking.

Technology

It's a basic fact that more technology is available to more people. I define *technology* as "anything that helps us do something." A pencil is technology, so is a scooter, so is a notebook computer or a cell phone.

Someone in Delhi who has a refrigerator with a water filter and ice-maker is enjoying the global spread of technology (and, some will point out, is suffering from the pollution resulting from manufacturing and running it). So is a Norwegian who clicks a ballpoint pen. In big cities anywhere, the ubiquitous cell phone is an obvious sign of the global spread of technology. A few decades ago we didn't have the technology to do some of the basic things we take for granted every day now. If you introduce a technology somewhere, such as a fleet of refrigerated trucks, this changes everything down to the locals' diet. The global spread of technology affects what we eat, how we get to work, what we do for work, what we wear, what we do for leisure, who we talk to and know, and uncountable other things.

Increased Media Exposure

Media (defined as film, television, radio, music CDs, videos, DVDs, advertisements, newspapers, books, magazines, Websites—anything you can read or hear) help people see "around the corner" to other parts of the earth more than ever before. The reader is certainly aware of what the increased speed and new types of media offer us for learning about world events and deeper ways of knowing about other people. The world is "shrinking" in the sense that we can more quickly and easily see how other people in other countries live. Unfortunately, the viewing seems to be happening mostly in one direction.

Media exposure should (but rarely does) go in both directions. That is, Americans should see the world, not just be seen by it. I insert here a gentle reminder to Americans that we must not be ethnocentric. Take media exposure for example: "They" (whoever "they" are —Germans, Chileans, Chinese) know more about *you* than you do about *them*. Don't be surprised when you meet Swedes who speak English with an American accent almost indistinguishable from your own. They may have been raised watching *Dallas* and *Starsky and Hutch* and they study English in school. Have *you* studied the Swedish language? What Swedish shows have you seen? Who runs the Swedish

Do they know more about you *than you know about* them?

government? Who are the French, Italian, Brazilian, or Austrian leaders? Okay...closer to home...who is the president of Mexico? The prime minister of Canada? The average person on the street in all of these places knows very well who the American president is. Study up! Learn more about *them*. It's more important than you know.

American "world" news is embarrassingly local. In most places outside the United States, international news is truly *international*, with significant time given to reports about a wide variety of countries and international issues. Even Canada has a significantly more outward focus than does the U.S.

We can perhaps partially (but not entirely) forgive Americans for being so locally focused, because the United States is so vast and geographically isolated. But we are also arrogant; many of us believe we are the biggest, best, smartest—and we have all the answers.

Lifestyle Choices

Increased media exposure can result in more lifestyle choices. As more products and gadgets become universally available, and more advertisers assault our eyes and ears promoting them, people can increasingly choose to live different lifestyles or visit different locales. As Americans tattoo Chinese characters or the yin and yang symbol on their ankles and shoulders, Asians ride on scooters with slogans (in English) such as "Freeway Feeling," "The Epochal Scooter," or "Join Us to Riding Joy." These are actual slogans I've seen on scooters! (There are more examples in the section on translators in Part 6.) We are charmed by what we see in other cultures, and the masses in most cultures are beginning to mimic each other in little ways such as these.

Americans are jealous of the Europeans, and Scandinavians in particular, for their generous vacation allowances, and a few Americans (count me solidly among them!) may actually be starting to live in a more "European" way by not continually working at a fever pitch.

The more we know about how other people live, speak, walk, dress, work, or play, the more we can emulate them if we so choose.

Telecommunications

If everyone seems to have a cell phone, they must be getting less expensive. Telecommunications costs have fallen. We've also gotten good at mass-producing tiny communication devices (cell phones with e-mail capability, laptop computers) that keep us connected.

The proponents of the argument that the Internet builds community say that the Internet brings people together because

Does the Internet build community or connectedness?

they can communicate with others and gain insights into other ways of life. The critics lament masses of isolated teenagers in their rooms clicking away on keyboards with sunlight only a distant memory.

I prefer the word *connectedness* to *community*. As I write this particular section, I am in an Internet café in Taipei. In this same time period, I have also prepared some e-mails. One is a response to a new business inquiry from someone in Canada. Another is to a colleague in the United States about an upcoming training program he will conduct. A third is to a friend back in the States. Yet another is to someone in Taipei who had a quick question about the work I am doing here. While the Internet may not offer me *community* with these people, I undoubtedly enjoy a valuable *connectedness* that is made possible because of telecommunications advances.

Speed

That the rate of change and the pace of life seem to be solidly on the increase is old news to anyone who is in touch with any form of media at all.

Computer chips double their speed every eighteen months. We can barely tolerate a computer that "bogs down" and takes nine seconds to complete a task—we need a faster one that can do the work twice as fast.

Sending an old-fashioned paper letter (remember those?) to another city takes two or three days. The recipient may need a day or two to respond, and then the reply will reach the original sender two or three days later. This five- or six-business-day cycle is now expected to be completed immediately owing to the advent of the fax machine and e-mail. This has raised the expectation of some cultures for speed-of-light turnaround times in business communication.

Some but not all cultures operate this way. Frenzied American workers who thrive on the success of fast-paced business must realize that the entire world does not operate on the same schedule. Many others thrive on the sound practice of moving more slowly. Still others savor the deliberateness of careful planning and looking before they leap. This means they may not give you an instant response to your e-mail. Not all cultures have embraced e-mail as much as the United States has. Others may not work late hours and weekends to meet a seemingly arbitrary deadline. They may not march to the same accelerated drumbeat that drives your business.

Whether all this increased speed is good or bad is certainly debatable, but it *is* a phenomenon spreading around the globe and it *is* undeniably a factor to consider in

> **"Fast" is neither good nor bad; it's just "fast."**

international business. For some, that means they must be careful not to overwhelm their slower-paced counterparts. For others, it means they need to accelerate or be left behind.

Advances in technology and exposure to the media have broadened our lifestyle choices and the speed with which we can conduct business. These basic factors have undeniably led to a shrinking of the business world. New business models that were not formerly possible are now becoming the norm.

Even tiny companies with some basic technical expertise and vision can operate around the clock, with a team working in India during the "night" and a team in California during the "day." The California team completes a day's work, goes home to sleep, then comes back to the office the next morning and finds that the project has been

With fewer trade barriers, culture becomes more important, not less important.

advanced another full workday by the team in India, who are now sleeping. Then, when the Indians arrive at the office the next morning, their work has been advanced another day while they slept. Following this method, in a five-day workweek, the company can advance a project "ten days."

If there is an urgent deadline to be met or a competitor to be beat, this is a very creative way of using technology and global time zones to great advantage. Of course, not everyone values a frenzied workplace and constant progress as much as Americans do, so it's reasonable to ask whether it's worth having your company open twenty-four hours a day.

But even for companies and individuals who work at a less intense pace, travel and telecommunications technologies have made the world smaller and cheaper to access. This of course has meant more opportunities for global trade.

At this writing, one of the largest American online computer sellers offers customer support through some 1,800 staff working in India. Many other companies operate on a similar model; it's cheaper to pay the long-distance phone charges, train the Indians in American or British culture and phone protocol, and pay the Indian salary levels than it is to run operations domestically. Whether individuals see them as detrimental or beneficial, new business models such as this will continue to emerge. When companies figure out such new ways to take further advantage of emerging technologies and the opportunities they present, the competition must either follow suit or fall behind.

Regional economies (such as the Asian economy) can certainly slow or crash. The global economy, too, is sluggish at times. The terrorist attacks of September 11, 2001, certainly made some Americans feel like isolating themselves. But in the big picture, and over time, global trade will inevitably increase.

One could very correctly argue that all of the technologies I mentioned above are mainly at the disposal of the First World and that there are hundreds of millions, even billions, of people who do not play an active role in global trade or enjoy the fruits of it.

Local > Regional > National > International > Global (*... > Extraterrestrial > Lunar > Interplanetary > Intersolar > Intergalactic > ???...*)

It's also quite reasonable to claim that global trade can lead to a greater division between rich and poor; there are those who argue against global trade *because* it exploits the poor of many countries.

Many companies that used to thrive locally eventually found they needed to go national to stay alive. If they were able to thrive nationally in the past, they are now finding it necessary to compete internationally. Now it seems the rule of the day is that businesses (and the people who run them) have to go global or go broke.

Economists may disagree about what will happen with global economics in the future, but I think we would be hard-pressed to find many who believe in its eventual demise. We have seen the economic and social advantages and disadvantages of globalization, and, like it or not, the trend is likely to continue.

So for now, let's stick with the reality of today, which is that American businesses *must* now compete with ever bigger global players and must think beyond U.S. borders if they are to hold their own against savvy emerging entities such as the expanding European Union or the Pacific Rim. Thinking and acting locally just don't cut it anymore.

Taking Your Business Global

Expanding your business to become a player in the global arena comes with its successes but also with its challenges. Too many companies try to grow internationally without a carefully crafted international strategy and are soon rudely awakened by the cultural problems they encounter.

A manager from one of America's best-known companies was a guest speaker in one of my grad school classes. After telling fantastic stories about how awestruck he was by the many cultural differences he encountered during his two years in Tokyo, a student asked him the following:

> **Student:** Would you recommend cross-cultural training for managers like you who are being transferred oveseas?
>
> **Manager:** Absolutely. I wouldn't let them leave home without it!
>
> **Student:** What training did (XYZ Company) provide you?
>
> **Manager:** Absolutely none.

Absolutely none!

Lots of people see with the perfect clarity of hindsight that "looking before you leap" internationally is a good idea. This manager did not fail on his assignment, and his company would certainly not have gone bankrupt if he had. But he saw clearly in hindsight that both he and his company would have benefited substantially from some cross-cultural training before he was sent abroad.

Companies can expand their business in a number of ways as they take that "leap" internationally. Here are six typical business strategies for going international:

1. Cross-border expansion: One company stretches its reach across a border or several borders. For example, you might decide to open a factory or a sales office in another country.

2. Mergers and acquisitions: One company purchases another or blends with it.

3. Joint ventures: Two companies start a new venture that exists as a third and separate entity. For example, Toyota and General Motors jointly formed a third company called Nummi, under shared ownership by both companies.

4. Strategic alliances: Companies stay separate but they agree to be sole distributors or exclusive suppliers for each other. For example, we are in different countries and I agree to buy all the raw materials to make sports equipment from you. You agree to give me exclusive access to the materials, and we both benefit from this cross-border arrangement.

5. International marketing and distribution: A company decides to directly sell its widgets in other countries.

6. International licensing: A company establishes local distributorships in other countries.

In all of these instances, culture is important. Cross-cultural interaction may be as limited as a few dozen phone calls between the United States and Canada, or it may involve several years of living in a country vastly different from your own.

With mergers and acquisitions, joint ventures, and strategic alliances (numbers 2, 3, and 4 above), there are two levels of potential culture clash: corporate culture and country culture. For example, when Chrysler (American) and Daimler-Benz (German) merged to become DaimlerChrysler, both corporations had very different company cultures (operating with different ways of establishing trust, interacting with superiors, motivating employees, and so forth) and also different national cultures to contend with and blend.

If domestic mergers, partnerships, or acquisitions are delicate operations prone to failure, it's easy to imagine that adding language barriers and international culture double or triple the problems. One expert in international expansion strategy, Dr. David Bastien, has suggested that the combined company- and country-culture clash can have profoundly negative results. He has described the following trends:

You'll do fine in Tokyo without any cross-cultural training, Ted! Just count to forty or so, then pull the ripcord.

- a 70–88 percent failure rate of international mergers and acquisitions

- a 65–80 percent failure rate of all (domestic or international) mergers, acquisitions, and change strategies (e.g., organizational changes such as moving to teams).

Bastien defines failure as follows:
- failure to meet expected financial goals
- divestiture (companies are often sold within two years of being acquired)
- bankruptcy (very rarely happens)
- acquisition of the parent company because it is vulnerable

And failure can take many milder forms:
- employees operating at reduced effectiveness
- low employee morale
- early return home of expatriates
- missed business opportunities due to cultural unfamiliarity
- loss of brand-name credibility due to culturally inappropriate marketing
- damage of company reputation due to actual or perceived ethical issues
- employee leaving the company in disgust

The Cost of Going International

The two levels of cultural clash (company and country) can contribute to all of the above dangers, and all of these reasons underscore the need for organizations to invest wisely in the most thorough and informed cross-cultural strategy possible.

Engaging in any form of international business is not inexpensive. Sending the manager from XYZ Company to Tokyo for two years certainly cost the company a pretty penny. Housing in Tokyo is difficult to find and very pricey. The company paid for storage of his household goods back in the United States while he was abroad, and it shipped a container of goods for his family to Tokyo (and of course back to the U.S. at the end of his assignment). He also received a salary increase as incentive as well as a cost-of-living add-on while he was in Tokyo. His family enjoyed the use of a company car in Japan, and the company had to pay the cost of flying him and his wife back to the U.S. several times during their time in Tokyo.

> **International business failures are expensive. So is international business success!**

The costs to relocate an individual or family overseas are estimated to be between $50,000 and $500,000, depending on such variables as the employee's position and salary, the country of destination, the length of assignment, the industry, the company or organiza-

Congratulations! You've just been acquired by a foreign company! After eighteen months of turmoil and backstabbing by co-workers, you'll be resold at a devastating loss to the highest bidder.

tion, the exchange rate, and various unpredictable developments during the assignment (wars, boycotts, strikes, terrorism, etc.).

The estimates skyrocket when you consider the fact that if the employee fails, you have to ship him (more "hims" than "hers" relocate overseas as expatriates) and his household back home and then prepare to send someone else (along with the new person's family and household goods) to take his place.

The basic question to ask is "How much are you willing to lose?" Personally, I would rather *invest* $50,000 in something than *lose* $5,000 in anything. If it were well spent, I would not regret investing the $50,000, but I would probably not soon forget losing the $5,000! Yet most companies fail to strategically invest a few thousand dollars in the right areas when they go international, and they end up losing, and sometimes losing many thousands, as a result.

Over and over again I see American companies that are successful locally but whose executives can't imagine any need at all for a planned, coherent international strategy as they begin to expand overseas. I don't waste my time or energy trying to sell my strategic consulting help to these people. Ironically, some of the biggest, most reputable companies are often blindsided because they do not operate with solid crosscultural strategy. Perhaps this is because some larger companies feel they can afford to lose a few hundred thousand dollars (or a few million dollars) or a few employees here and there.

Other companies do see the need for international and cross-cultural strategies and training, but many of them try to do this in-house when they are seriously underqualified to do it right. I liken this to

You're not pulling your weight around here, Fred. We're sending you to the Hong Kong office for a few years.

saying, "Nah—we don't need the fire department. We handle all our firefighting *in-house.*" Well, that strategy may work for a small fire that needs only a small fire extinguisher...but bigger fires need bigger resources. If you're aiming low internationally and if you're planning to stay small, then by all means take care of cross-cultural preparation in-house. But if you're planning on a serious, and seriously successful, international strategy, plan on investing some significant resources and effort to understanding the cultures you're planning to enter. Give yourself an advantage.

"Wait! Don't call the fire department. We handle all our problems in-house around here..."

It's important to remember that not only do international business failures cost more money than most companies expect, but so do international successes!

Cultural Differences Will Always Matter

Above I've described a number of ways in which the world is shrinking and becoming connected in faster, less expensive ways. I've also discussed the necessity for going international with your business. The most difficult aspect of going global isn't, however, learning to take advantage of the rapid shrinking of the world through technology, communications, the media, and so forth. It is dealing with cultural differences.

The general idea of having a "meeting" is understood around the world, as is the importance of negotiation. The way we do business in various countries, from technologies to company structures, seems to be pretty "universal"—at first glance. But while these "big picture," surface concepts are understood around the globe, the mental processes and rules for interacting in business or in life are not. The way people interact face to face in business meetings, the way they greet

> **Newsflash!**
> **Despite major changes in Japan in the last fifty years, the Japanese remain Japanese!**

in the morning in the office, the level of formality they choose when addressing co-workers, the language they speak when they want to relate to a work colleague quickly, the degree of directness they deem appropriate in team conflicts, the jokes they tell or don't tell with co-workers, the reason they feel comfortable or uncomfortable with another person—all these "little things" are ways in which cultures maintain their uniqueness.

Such "little things" are in fact very "big." They are important because they are what can make or break a deal; they are what can sweeten or sour business relations. And they are pervasive. Together they make a bigger picture.

By way of analogy, consider a seemingly unimportant behavior, such as whether someone smokes or how he or she chews or uses a fork or what he or she eats. These are certainly of no consequence in the big picture. Yet face to face at a table (which is how business often happens) they can be very important (annoying or delightful). In the long term, they can end a life or break up a couple. And they may be very difficult to change. The little stuff really does count, and it's safe to say it will never go away. We are kidding ourselves if we think cultural differences will disappear. In fact, I would never want them to disappear! I would be horrified if the Italians had their Italianness bleached out of them! May the Argentineans always remain Argentinean!

Yes, media, technology, and transportation continue to shrink the world and even unify it in some ways, but cultural differences will never disappear. Instead, more and more of these differences will become apparent as we are increasingly exposed to them and interact with cultural others. So in an increasingly accessible world, cultures play a *bigger*, not a *smaller* role in business. Cultural intelligence becomes *more* important, not *less* important.

Certainly, the idea of a "single earth culture" is not in the cards. The Japanese will remain Japanese,

> **In our shrinking world, culture becomes more important, not less important.**

the French will remain French, and the Americans will remain Americans. And if you make the mistake of thinking the French are Americanized, try calling a few of the French "American" and see what happens. (And be ready to duck out of the way before they give you the verbal beating about the ears you deserve!)

Part 3

What Is Cultural Intelligence?

The use of the term *cultural intelligence* is widespread. A Web search will find scores of pages containing the exact term *cultural intelligence*. Maybe it's because the term is in such common use that several attempts to register it as a trademark have failed. Nobody owns the term or the concept behind it; certainly nobody holds any kind of monopoly on it. The term has been used in military settings, by non-profit organizations, and by companies, consultants, and so forth. It has been interpreted in myriad ways.

I first used *cultural intelligence* in a training program in the late 1980s, and I'm sure it was coined before I started introducing it back then. I am glad that the term is widely used today.

What about the term *cultural competence*, which is also in wide use? I shy away from the term *competence* because it's not something we should ultimately strive for but rather, should excel beyond. Imagine an employee performance review or letter of recommendation in which you are described merely as competent. What an insult (especially to Americans, who prefer overstatement rather than understatement)! In some fields, such as medicine, incompetence can be clearly recognized. In others, such as academics, it cannot always be detected. It follows that doctors carry malpractice insurance, but professors do not (though some perhaps should). While competence suggests meeting at least basic minimum requirements, intelligence suggests more highly developed abilities. So rather than dealing with competence versus incompetence, I propose people take on the higher goal of demonstrating cultural *intelligence*, which might imply some savvier insights and wiser actions.

Defining Cultural Intelligence

In Part 1 I discussed how the word *culture* is used widely and with multiple interpretations. As I begin to define and examine *cultural intelligence* as it relates to this book, I will first point out that the word *intelligence*, like the word *culture*, is subject to numerous interpretations as well as considerable debate and controversy.

People disagree about how IQ should be measured and whether it can be increased. Some question the validity of standardized IQ tests because they may contain cultural bias (an IQ test with a picture of a coal scuttle or a story including mittens will certainly be confusing to people who know nothing about coal furnaces and who live in climates where there is no need for mittens).

Another potential difficulty with the concept of intelligence stems from the fact that it is quantifiable against a standard (resulting in an "IQ score"). Scores or grades can be perceived as having a sense of permanency to them; this can sometimes be problematic when such labels lead people to believe that intelligence can be boiled down to an IQ score. Imagine that you are of at least average intelligence but you take an IQ test that wrongly pegs you as "below average" (maybe it was a bad day when you took the test). You may wear that albatross around your neck your entire life. I would much rather see a person obtain a false *high* score on an IQ test and then spend the rest of his or her life believing (and acting like) the label fits!

I propose that we focus on defining and then increasing cultural intelligence quotient (CQ), not measuring it. What's the point,

You've got a CQ of 149!

after all, of walking around announcing, *"I've got a CQ of 149!"*? I don't use catchy initials such as "CQ" either, because I want to avoid falling into the oversimplification trap that can be a risk any time one labels a complicated concept.

While there is no one correct definition of *cultural intelligence*, some readers may find it helpful to see some kind of written definition, so let's begin with this one:

> *Cultural intelligence is the ability to engage in a set of behaviors that uses skills (i.e., language or interpersonal skills) and qualities (e.g., tolerance for ambiguity, flexibility) that are tuned appropriately to the culture-based values and attitudes of the people with whom one interacts.*

Several concepts contribute to the various parts of the definition above. The material in this part examines those and helps you through the process of learning how to increase your cultural intelligence.

Multiple Intelligences Theory Factors In

The psychologist Howard Gardner started people thinking differently about intelligence. He coined the term *multiple intelligences* and suggested that there is more to being intelligent than the logical, verbal, or mathematical intelligence typically measured on standard IQ tests. For example, a musician might be a genius on the piano but have very low math or verbal skills. It would be wrong to label a musician as "not intelligent" because of a low score on an IQ test. A dancer or a karate master might have great skills relating to movement and space but might know nothing about a piano. A genius on an IQ test may not stand a chance when sparring with a karate master. The basic idea is that there's more than one way to be smart, and Gardner offers some useful categories for defining intelligence.

Here are Gardner's categories of multiple intelligences and the occupations that are the most closely aligned with each.

Measured by standard IQ tests:

1. Linguistic (language teachers, interpreters, and editors)

2. Logical–mathematical (computer programmers, accountants, and scientists)

Not measured by standard IQ tests:

3. Spatial (engineers, surgeons, sculptors, and painters)

4. Musical (Mozart, Hendrix, Pavarotti)

5. Body/kinesthetic (dancers, athletes, and surgeons)

6. Interpersonal (salespeople, politicians, teachers, negotiators, and capable leaders)

7. Intrapersonal (authors, actors, inventors, and entrepreneurs)

In 1995, Daniel Goleman put forth the idea of *emotional intelligence*, or "EQ." In very simple terms, I see emotional intelligence as similar to Gardner's intrapersonal intelligence. It means knowing who you are, being centered, balanced, in touch. We have a lesson to learn from Gardner and Goleman when we consider cultural intelligence.

I propose that *cultural intelligence* is a unique and vital thread that runs through (and then beyond) various aspects of multiple intelligences theory and emotional intelligence theory, especially in the following four areas: linguistic, spatial, intrapersonal (or emotional), and interpersonal intelligences.

Linguistic Intelligence

Interacting successfully with people from other cultures whose native language is not English requires language skills. The salesperson who can interact with clients in the clients' native language has a much better chance of charming them and closing the sale. The customer service person or front-desk receptionist who can speak even a little bit of his or her customers' native language stands a better chance of making a positive impression than one who cannot. Consider the opposite: how would you feel if someone you were going to buy something from couldn't even pronounce the name of your city correctly or, more importantly, couldn't pronounce your name correctly? (In a sense, a person's name is the most important thing you can know about an individual!)

The more you are involved with your international counterparts, the wiser it is for you to learn as much as possible of their language. What higher compliment can you pay a business partner than to demonstrate a genuine interest in something so personal as his or her native language by making the effort to learn it? And what greater insult can there be than not bothering to learn even a modicum of it?

Some argue that everyone worldwide speaks English and there is therefore no reason to learn foreign languages. Wrong. Although it's true that many do speak English, it's only because they have invested significant time and money to learn it. But your knowing something about your international counterparts' or customers' native language remains important; foreign language proficiency may not be necessary for you to communicate, but it can give you an undeniable edge over your competitors.

Linguistic intelligence can also be demonstrated even if English is the only language used. You can be more successful if you know how to effectively use what I call

> **You don't have to speak a second language fluently to have cultural intelligence.**

"international business English." There are tips for doing this in Part 6. I also suggest specific strategies in Part 6 to help you make the most of a second language, even with a limited vocabulary.

Spatial Intelligence

Spatial intelligence is probably the most straightforward of those that I propose as being important components of cultural intelligence. When we interact with people from other cultures, at a minimum we should know the proper behaviors to help us get through an introduction, a business meeting, a meal, or other scenarios without making fools of ourselves. In this context spatial intelligence relates to simple things such as how close people stand to one another in conversation, where the most important person sits at a meeting, how chairs are arranged, whether people bow or shake hands or touch each other, and the ability to understand and anticipate and sometimes appropriately imitate body language.

For example, when South American men talk to me, they sometimes pat me firmly on the upper arm or shoulder to show friendliness or closeness. When we shake hands, they may use two hands to show more warmth and sincerity.

Nothing remotely like this has happened to me in Asia. If I patted an Asian man on the arm or shoulder the way South Americans have done to me to show closeness, it would definitely not bring us closer or build trust in any way! In contrast, Asians have adeptly shown me courtesy by opening doors for me, bowing slightly, stepping back out of the way so I can pass into the room first, and so on. South Americans would probably find it ridiculous if I showed such obsequious behaviors around them.

Here's an example relating to space: Americans do not hesitate to sprawl in their chairs or put their feet up on train benches. This makes sense considering that the United States is a vast country with wide-open spaces; our cars, streets, houses, and refrigerators are all bigger than almost anywhere else. When Americans sit or stand or make gestures, they take up more space than most others.

In a typical interaction, a Colombian graduate student approached me during a break in the first session of a class I was teaching. He had the syllabus in his hand and wanted to ask a question about it. As he talked to me, he stood much closer than I would have chosen to stand to anyone in that kind of situation. As you might guess, I stood my ground because I knew that if I backed up to leave more space, he might close the distance again and we might end up tangoing across the floor.

The various ways of using body, voice, or space are not inherently good or bad; they merely represent differences. The ability or failure to adapt our spatial behaviors can make our international counterparts comfortable or ill at ease, which in turn can contribute to various levels of success or failure in face-to-face cross-cultural interactions.

Intrapersonal Intelligence

Of the four of Gardner's intelligences that contribute most to cultural intelligence, intrapersonal intelligence risks being the most nebulous. But what I mean here is basic: you need to know your own cultural style. If you are aware of your own cultural style, you can more easily compare yourself with others, and you will then be able to adjust your behavior to be compatible in cross-cultural settings.

Self-awareness as an aspect of cultural intelligence could be based on all of the categories and themes that I touch on in various parts of the book. In the Introduction I shared my perception that most people may see themselves as "cultureless," when actually everyone has a culture. I also suggest debunking this myth in Part 5 when I address the question, "What Is Your Cultural Style?" In my work and research, I have found that people are rarely aware of how the bigger themes (the part of the iceberg that is under the water) relates to their own culture.

> **When studying others' cultures under a magnifying glass, don't forget to use a mirror and examine your own culture.**

Knowing yourself is of course a lifelong lesson involving constant practice and evolution. I find it difficult to offer general advice in this category beyond encouraging people to keep learning about themselves, because every person is unique in many ways.

Interpersonal Intelligence

Successful interaction with people from other cultures is the heart of cultural intelligence. Knowing facts about another culture is helpful, but your approach can't be only academic or intellectual; you need to know how to interact successfully with people. Do you charm people from other cultures or do you turn them off? Can you modify your behaviors in appropriate ways when you are with clients or colleagues from various cultures?

Gardner suggests that interpersonal intelligence is the ability to respond appropriately to others. He cites Helen Keller's teacher Anne Sullivan as an example of an individual with the ability to reach out and communicate with someone even when the use of language was not possible. Though Helen Keller's blindness and deafness represent extreme communication barriers, those in cross-cultural interactions face not entirely dissimilar challenges due to the difficulties when the two sides do not share a common language, communication style, or worldview. I'm not exaggerating with this comparison; I see it as a useful metaphor for cross-cultural interactions, but I encourage you to recognize the ways in which not only your international counterparts but especially *you* may be metaphorically somewhat blind or deaf to cultural differences.

Gardner further suggests that interpersonal intelligence is something beyond the language aspects of communication and beyond communication itself. He describes interpersonal intelligence as the ability to "read the intentions and desires of others, even when they have been hidden." Gardner explains that this skill may be highly developed in therapists, teachers, and political leaders (among others). The ability to "read" people and anticipate their motivations and desires is an aspect of interpersonal intelligence that is crucial to professionals in international interactions. This is the skill of the emergency room doctor who can deduce what is wrong or what a family desires, in spite of language barriers. This is the skill of the international sales representative who can anticipate what will close a sale when negotiating with people from other cultures.

This is another area where general advice is difficult to give, because human interactions are unpredictable and there are limitless specific scenarios in which intercultural relationships are enhanced or diminished.

Perhaps the best way to coach you toward increasing this aspect of cultural intelligence is to suggest that you closely examine your motivation for learning about other cultures. I have noticed, especially since September 11, 2001, that more Americans are asking, "Can't we all just get along?" and "Why do they hate us?" By broadening our worldview and learning how others perceive us, we will begin to appreciate the reasons why others may feel uncomfortable with us. I highly doubt that the September 11, 2001, terrorists considered themselves or their act as *evil* any more than the American leadership considered itself evil for the subsequent American-led war against Iraq a few years later. There was worldwide outrage against both actions. Yet almost certainly a small number of actors on both sides were firmly under the impression that their cause was noble and their intentions were good. The U.S. has been articulately and legitimately criticized, from without and within, for exercising military and business might. While individual citizens may not have any say over general United States military policy or American business practices, each of us can work to improve relations at the individual level. This is impossible without first understanding what motivates people other than ourselves. Upon this understanding can then be built the skills of successful interaction.

I first lived abroad as a teenager during the time when the United States was bombing Libya. On foreign news broadcasts I saw coverage of President Reagan being burned in effigy, of American flags burning, and of Libyans gathered in the street chanting and shooting machine guns into the air. I'm not sure if this was my first exposure to such images due to my youth or because of different reporting practices by U.S. media, but my eyes were opened for the first time to the reality that the U.S. is not automatically and universally well liked or respected everywhere. It motivated me to do all I could to enjoy the best possible relationships and interactions with people from other countries.

Whether the motive is to work for peace or for profit or for international understanding, we must find our own reason for developing our interpersonal intelligence across cultures.

I find that Gardner's multiple intelligences theory offers some simple but rich categories for examining cultural intelligence. My focus on the above four of Gardner's categories could be boiled down to this extremely oversimplified sentence: *To interact well with people from other cultures, it helps to (a) speak a bit of their language, (b) know how closely to stand (and other nonverbal behavior), (c) know about your own cultural style, and (d) know how your cultural style meshes with those of others.*

Considering all four of these categories is a good start toward defining cultural intelligence, but more than these categories of skill areas is needed, and the next section expands our definition of cross-cultural intelligence by describing the characteristics of the culturally intelligent professional.

The Culturally Intelligent Professional

Haven't we all encountered people who are good at the various skills required by their work but who are not happy with their job and are perhaps a bit "unpleasant" to work with? I have known people who are skilled but who probably would not do well overseas simply because they prefer the comforts (physical and psychological) of staying home. Naturally, part of cultural intelligence must involve some kind of willingness—and intention—to do well in international situations. So, characteristics such as open-mindedness or the desire to try new things are also important parts of the cultural intelligence equation. Following is a table with various traits that can lead to greater cultural intelligence. How would you rank yourself?

How do you rank yourself?	Needs improve-ment	Strength	Significant Strength
Open-mindedness			
Flexibility with attitudes and behavior			
Ability to adapt your behavior			
Appreciation of differences			
Comfort with uncertainty			
Ability to trust when dealing with the unfamiliar			
Win-win attitude			
Humility			
Extroversion			
Creativity			
Tactfulness			
Willingness to have your own views challenged			
Ability to make independent decisions when you are far from your usual resources			
Being invigorated by differ-ences			
Ability to see a familiar situa-tion from unfamiliar vantage points			
Patience when you are not in control			
Ability to deal with the stress of new situations			
Sensitivity to nuances of dif-ferences			
Respect for others			

Continued...

How do you rank yourself?	Needs improvement	Strength	Significant Strength
Willingness to change yourself as you learn and grow (versus changing others to fit you)			
Empathy			
Sense of humor			

How did you rank yourself on the above table? How would you rank your colleagues? How would they rank you? The above table can be used as a tool for 360-degree feedback; see if you and your colleagues agree with how you rank yourselves and one another.

These characteristics are some that experienced international businesspeople in my cross-cultural programs and throughout my cross-cultural career have reported to me as being particularly useful in international mixes, both domestic and overseas. Other international business writers and researchers propose similar lists and include other sets of traits.

Some of these characteristics are useful in *any* setting, but they become even more important when you are working in an internationally mixed environment because more of these traits are likely to be required of you simultaneously than in any other setting. And you are less likely to be able to predict what will happen next to tax your patience or require you to be flexible.

Let's consider an example from the list—humility—and see how it might be more important in international mixes. In your own country you can do just about anything you need for daily living and for work. You know where to buy stamps, you know how much gas costs and the places you prefer to buy it, you know how to get groceries or any household supplies you need, and you know how to do the various functions of your job. In an overseas setting, all this familiarity vanishes and you are left feeling not quite so confident. You might command an entire department or division in an important company at home, but abroad you can't even buy a stamp or find your way to a gas station. This is naturally humbling. Those who go brashly crashing through foreign lands without humility are at risk of being perceived as Ugly Americans (or

Ugly Japanese, etc.). Humility and the ability to change from the role of expert to the role of learner suddenly become distinct advantages in international settings.

The need for humility can also arise in international interactions in your home country. I suppose you could go brazenly bumbling through interactions with international clients or customers at home, but this is no way to gain trust or keep business. If you want to market your services or products to the Latino community at home, for instance, you'd better not only understand Latino sensibilities but also respect Latinos. Knowing about them, interacting with them, and keeping them as customers require more effort than dealing with the mainstream. Because it involves more learning and more exposure to the unfamiliar, you can't be cocky experts at dealing with Latinos or Asian Americans or foreign personnel even in your own country, and you would do well to approach the situation with humility. Unless your international customers have nowhere to turn but to you, you risk losing them to the competition if you don't treat them with respect and humility.

Can Cultural Intelligence Be Increased?

I've seen lots of tests, including IQ tests, with varieties of puzzles and problems, and I know that it's possible to learn how to take these tests and improve my score. I've also interacted with people from lots of cultures, within the setting of their own cultures, and I know it's possible to improve interpersonal relations skills. There's nothing wrong with "studying for the test" when your business is at stake, pass or fail.

Appropriate conduct in a mixed-culture business meeting can be learned, as can many other cross-cultural skills. A significant industry has emerged to train businesspeople and other professionals in intercultural awareness and sensitivity. Such training, along with reading on your own (see Recommended Readings for suggested books), can help you increase your cultural intelligence.

Don't make the mistake of thinking that your cultural intelligence cannot decrease. Yes, it can slip! Ask most people who studied a second language in college how much of it they can speak today.

> **Don't make the mistake of thinking that your cultural intelligence is "fixed" and cannot be increased.**

New and existing intercultural skills, just like a foreign language, must be practiced to be retained.

Gaining Cultural Intelligence—a Process

Earlier I used the example of juggling to propose that we need to increase not only our awareness and our knowledge but also our skills to truly learn something about cultures. Increasing your cultural intelligence takes time, just as learning to juggle does. Consider your current job and all the skills it requires. You were of course hired, not born, into the organization you work for, and it took you time to build familiarity with it and to be effective. You have learned a variety of things, right down to where the memo pads are kept and where you can get something photocopied.

Remember the seemingly overwhelming amount of information you had to absorb as a new employee in order to function as you do in your job? The process of building cultural intelligence is similar. People who arrive in a new country where they will be staying for an extended time typically want to know everything and want to be able to do everything immediately. Wouldn't it be nice to be able to accomplish everything in one week—from establishing your new telephone service to making new friends to learning how to conduct a meeting with new cultural rules?

Unfortunately (or fortunately!), it doesn't work that way. Even though it's sometimes frustrating, I think it's fortunate that life and learning aren't easy. One of the first things I enjoy doing when I arrive in a foreign city is exploring the streets in bigger and bigger concentric circles, starting from my hotel or my base. Even if I could have a city map or navigation system magically zapped into my head, I wouldn't want that! The messy, tedious process of getting to know a place is what makes me remember it and get to like it. The same is even truer of people, languages, and cultural differences.

Many Ways to View the World

One of the ways people inevitably increase their awareness when learning about other cultures is to move from thinking "My way is the only way" toward thinking "There are many valid ways" of interpreting and participating in life. And the process involves more than changing your thinking; it also involves adjusting your behaviors.

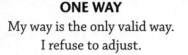

ONE WAY

My way is the only valid way.

I refuse to adjust.

MANY WAYS

There are many valid ways.

I am prepared to adjust.

Of course culture plays a major role in how people participate in and interpret the world and life, and the more you explore other cultural viewpoints and practices, the more you will see that there are multiple valid perspectives.

It's natural to start out somewhere toward the left side of the scale above, because you know only your own worldview until you see that of others. But do you stay toward the left of the scale, or do you move toward the right? That's the critical question.

As you learn, evolve, and gain perspective, it becomes possible for you to move toward the right of this scale. I say it's possible and, as you might guess, I think it's desirable. But it's not at all guaranteed. My optimistic side would say that it's natural for your mind to open as you learn more about others. But as you experience more of life, it's also natural to find things you prefer and others you dislike. Those preferences and dislikes can become fossilized. Couldn't happen to you, you claim? Have you ever found yourself thinking, "Oh, I'd *never* drive a Chevrolet!" (or "Oh, I *only* drive Chevrolets!"). I think it's natural to stop looking for solutions and new perspectives when you feel you've figured out how things work and how to get through life in a way that satisfies you. Just as you don't keep looking for your car keys after you've found them, your natural tendency might be to stop looking at other cultural perspectives when you think you've got a perfectly work-able cultural style and way of interpreting the world. In fact, I might go further and say that when we think we've found the answers, we might naturally be highly resistant to anything that challenges those comfortable answers.

I will admit that my bias, or my point of departure, in thinking about cultures is that multiple perspectives and the ability to adjust to multiple ways of life are desirable. But I am not blindly optimistic to the extent that I think people want to naturally expand their world-view; it can be a difficult process. I believe that to successfully progress toward the right on the scale requires deliberate and conscious effort.

How you get there (assuming you want to) is up to you. What I will do below is examine ways for describing what happens to us as we move from the left to the right on this scale. There are other theories that can contribute to the discussion of this process, but for simplicity's sake, I offer very brief discussions of only three of them.

Intellectual and Ethical Development

The psychologist William Perry proposes the following framework to describe the evolution of our thought processes, and here's how I would apply it to the "One way/Many ways" scale above.

Dualism—We only see the world in black and white terms. For example, this could mean "our way" versus "their way," the "American way" versus the "Swedish way," or the "capitalist way" versus the "communist way." This level of development would be located close to the left end of scale. At this phase, we would not be willing to change our behaviors toward what we perceived as an inferior way. Further to the left, perhaps even off the scale, is the stage where people do not even see the existence of other ways. This is where people might innocently believe "My way is the only way."

Multiplicity—As we move toward the right on the scale, we begin to acknowledge that there are diverse perspectives and begin to accept some of them. If we have not progressed very far to the right, this stage can look like dualism if we quickly abandon our original perspectives and adopt or idealize some new perspective. In plain English, this is what happens when people travel abroad and "go native"; an American might discover the Italian way of life, decide it's wonderful, and have nothing but negatives to say about the American way of life. New perspectives can be recognized as legitimate at this stage, but the view that one way is better than another can persist.

Relativism—Shifting further to the right, we accept that there are multiple ways of seeing the world and living life. Here we can appreciate other cultures and all that they entail. At this stage we can recognize multiple perspectives as being valid and are not likely to negatively evaluate a cultural trait without careful thought.

Committed relativism—Finally, at the right end of the scale, the most advanced stage, not only do we see that there are multiple valid ways of living and thinking, but we are able to make an informed decision about what ways are best for us. We recognize that other ways may be better for other people, and in fact we may understand exactly why they are better within certain cultural contexts, but we can commit knowingly to ways that make sense within our own lives and our own cultural context.

Milton Bennett has aptly applied Perry's thinking to cross-cultural issues using the labels "ethnocentrism" (toward the left) and "committed ethnorelativism" (on the right).

Lawrence Kohlberg proposes seven stages of moral development that relate to how people make decisions about right and wrong; these could be applied to the "One way/Many ways" scale. On the left would be Kohlberg's lowest stages, where we think in terms of right and wrong, good and bad, and rules. This is not unrelated to Perry's dualism and the idea that cultures can be seen as black and white. In terms of our cultural intelligence discussion, this is where we would label other cultural perspectives as bad, backward, even abnormal.

Moving toward the middle, Kohlberg's stages involve decision making based on societal pressures and the desire to fit in with social norms. In other words, we decide what is right or wrong based on how other people might perceive us. This can only happen with the realization that there are such social norms to conform to and an awareness that others can perceive us and make judgments about us. This could be related to Perry's multiplicity stage. Cultural intelligence is somewhat increased here in that we have at least a beginning awareness, if not acceptance, of others.

On the right, we might be able to slot Kohlberg's highest stages, where people make informed decisions autonomously after considering multiple perspectives. This would not be dissimilar to Perry's committed relativism in that we choose our own solution after considering other options.

Whether you relate more to the terminology of Perry, Bennett, Kohlberg, or someone else, the basic idea is that development of cultural intelligence entails moving from left to right on the "One way/Many ways" scale: (1) from black and white thinking and the refusal or inability to accept other ways (2) to dealing in gray areas and being open to differences (3) to being able to adapt successfully in any cultural environment (4) to, finally, making informed decisions of our own.

Attitude and Behavior Change

What we are changing as we move from the left to the right is at question here. As I proposed in the juggling metaphor, we can learn *about* something or we can learn to actually *do* it. Of course most learning will involve some level of both. I propose that we have to challenge our thinking (our attitudes and values in the much bigger bottom portion of the cultural iceberg from Part 1) before we can change our behaviors (which are above the waterline of the cultural iceberg).

The simple point here is that the process of learning about other cultures first involves learning about new attitudes and values, but eventually we must put them into practice by adapting our behavior to fit our cultural environment—abroad or with internationals at home.

Toward the left of the "One way/Many ways" scale we may become aware of different attitudes and values, and as we move toward the right, we can accordingly practice changing our behavior in ways that allow us to operate effectively in other cultures and/or with people from other cultures.

To tie in Perry's concept of "committed relativism": at the right end of the scale we would see that there are many legitimate culture-based values to choose from, we would know clearly what our own culture-based values are, and we would be able to adjust our behaviors appropriately to be effective within a given cultural context. The previous sentence is quite close to the definition of cultural intelligence that I offered at the beginning of Part 3 on page 89.

The Cultural Adjustment Process

The simple point I want to make here is that no matter how you define cultural intelligence for your own professional circumstances and according to your own development, working toward it is a process, not an instant fix.

You might have picked up the impression that I'm pretty optimistic about other languages and cultures and that I embrace opportunities to learn about them. That's mostly true—most of the time. But I will confess here that I sometimes dread the process, and I dread it because of my familiarity with culture shock.

Everyone is familiar with the term *culture shock*. I don't like the expression because it implies a jolt or sudden zap of some sort. It might better be called "culture ache" or "culture blues," because it often comes from the long and frustrating process of adjusting to another culture. There are, in fact, predictable cycles of ups and downs that people go through when they relocate to other cultures. Just as you don't increase your cultural intelligence overnight, you don't experience all the frustration of international living or intercultural interactions overnight either.

Of the places outside the United States I've traveled, lived, or worked, I have spent the most time so far in France, and I'm quite familiar with the French and French culture. French is the language I speak most fluently (after English). In spite of these facts, each time I travel to France I am frustrated for some new reason. I have done plenty of muttering and grumbling to myself while living in France because it has seemed to me that whether I'm setting up a bank account or asking to buy something, the French seem to start with "*Non*" or "*C'est impossible*" and then slowly move toward "Yes" and "I guess that will be possible." Americans often do the opposite;

"Culture shock" should be called "culture blues"

they start by thinking that anything is possible (the can-do people) and then try their hardest to find a way of accomplishing the impossible. Once it took me eleven days to set up a certain type of bank account in France. I later timed it on a stopwatch and found that it took me eleven *minutes* to set up a similar account in the U.S.

The list of frustrations I have had in various countries could go on and on. I have been irritated by the clogs of scooters and the air pollution in Asian cities, the resigned acceptance of violence and extreme poverty in Brazil, the "strange telephone system" in (well, in any variety of places!).

When I find myself muttering about things like this and missing things from home such as the efficient American banking system, the scooter-free streets, or the familiar and easy telephone system, it helps me to remember that I am experiencing the cultural adjustment process. Though I have had my glimpses of the right end of the One way/Many ways scale, it's in those moments that I realize most I am always at risk of slipping back toward the left end, toward Perry's dualism stage of development.

At those times, I try to remind myself that the French way of being cautious with risks and of engaging people in argument and dialogue works wonderfully in France, and scooters are the *perfect* way to commute in densely populated tropical cities where it never snows, and every country's telephone system is, quite logically, the right (or at least the best possible) telephone system for that country at that time.

If I can see things that way, I am more able to accept the fact that there are many valid ways of living, working, talking, being, and doing. I might not choose to do things that way in my own culture, but I can certainly see why things are done that way in another.

The process of increasing your cultural intelligence is just that, a *process*. It is sometimes analogous to walking uphill in sand: two steps forward, one step back.

To close this part on a step forward, I will encourage you to stick to the process of increasing your cultural intelligence and recognize that it involves ups and downs, moving forward and sliding back, no matter who you are, no matter which culture you are dealing with, and regardless of whether you are dealing with it in "their" country or your own. I believe that, as with any learning experience, the enrichment you find at the end does justify the toil of getting there. And as with any journey, getting there can be half the fun if you can just remember that it should be!

Part 4

Applying Cultural Intelligence in Daily Work and Life

The five culture scales presented in Part 1 are intended as a beginning structure to help you become aware of the cultural differences you may face on a regular basis. Now we will zoom in and take a closer look at some more specific types of cultural dimensions (as represented by more scales) and learn how our lives, especially our work lives, are governed by our own cultural orientations and those of others.

Before we begin our exploration of cultural dimensions, though, for those of you who are wondering, "Why do I have to go through all of those dimensions? Can't I just have a list for each culture of the things I should and shouldn't do?" Here's why a simple list of dos and don'ts won't work very well.

Dos and Don'ts Are a Don't

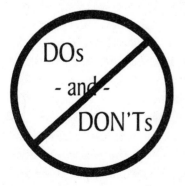

There are numerous books, articles, and quizzes detailing some pretty funny "dos and don'ts" that we may encounter at the tip of the iceberg and that we should supposedly follow when we conduct international business. I recall one "don't" story about an American (I think she was in Thailand) who received a set of "beads" as a gift at a party. She graciously thanked her hosts and put the beads around her neck. She immediately sensed that something was wrong, and indeed she later learned that the beads were some kind of underwear or lingerie.

I'm sure that particular woman will never make that *particular* mistake again in that particular situation in that particular country. And I'm also sure that 99.44 percent of the people reading this book will never deal with that particular situation, but rest assured there will be many equivalent ones awaiting you.

Memorizing a long list of dos and don'ts won't really help you much on specific occasions, nor in the long run with the important business and interactional matters that count.

There are two problems with relying solely on dos and don'ts. First, the list of dos and don'ts you memorize for one country won't necessarily apply when you cross the border into another country. Your Japanese dos and don'ts won't get you far in Singapore (and will certainly apply even less in Italy). The second problem with dos and don'ts is that there are simply too many to memorize to cover the thousands of hypothetical situations you could find yourself in.

Still, we need to know how to behave in other cultures. Many Americans learn, for example, that they should present business cards to their Japanese associates with two hands and say *"Hajima mashite"* (meaning "Pleased to meet you," but we will probably never pronounce it quite perfectly). We are sometimes told we might want to bow (just enough but not too deeply—and we never get that quite right either). We are also well advised not to shove the card in our back pocket or to write on it. Writing on a business card defaces it.

It's true that trying to say "Hajima mashite" may charm the Japanese and show them we are indeed pleased to meet them and we care enough about their language to at least try learning a bit of it. But instead of seeing this as an item in a list of dos and don'ts, consider the general principle behind the act: when you exchange cards with a

Japanese businessperson, you show respect for the card and for the person. Across Asia people show respect by handing papers to someone with two hands. If you were handling a valuable document, you wouldn't casually extend it to someone using one hand.

When you use two hands, you show that you are handling the paper more respectfully. Leaning forward to give someone something with two hands takes a little extra effort; it may almost put a little strain on your back, since you need to lean your whole torso forward. This is a way of "putting yourself out" for the other person, of doing something special.

You might want to take a few extra seconds to look at the card or even read it out loud to show that you are genuinely interested in it. "Ah! 'Manager of Sales,'" you might say to acknowledge the person's title, which is an indication of another under-the-waterline cultural trait: the importance of status and role. This could also be a good opportunity to see if you can pronounce the person's name correctly. His name (most often, it will be a man in Japan) is the most important thing you can know about that person.

These little signs of respect don't usually enter the minds of Westerners. For us, a business card is just a practical, concise way of transferring contact information and remembering a name and possibly a position, not a symbol of the self.

This business card discussion is one example of how we're better off knowing a general principle (respect, status) rather than memorizing specific dos and don'ts and mechanically performing them. This business card discussion is not unrelated to the same factors that are operating when some of my international students hand me clean, crisp, well-presented papers while the American students often toss theirs on my desk with rumpled and creased pages.

Some of the dimensions in this part might fit clearly within one of the five culture scales of Part 1; some of them may fit in several scales;

some may fall mostly outside them; but all relate to issues that can affect an internationally mixed work environment at home or abroad.

For example, the first issue in this part, "Role of Managers," could relate to the first culture scale from Part 1, "Equality versus Hierarchy." Or it could relate to the third scale, "Individual versus Group," because the decisions made by managers may be more collaborative in group cultures and more command style in individual cultures.

As you read through the material in this part and apply it to your work, you may find that your company culture has a stronger influence than your national culture. For example, a military unit will follow a command style of decision making in any country.

Location on the scales in this part also varies according to specific situations. For example, if you are formulating a five-year company plan, you may choose to follow a slower, more inclusive decision-making process. But if a fire erupted in your office, you wouldn't want to sit around asking each person for input on what to do. One would grab a fire extinguisher, another would call the fire department, another would ring the fire alarm, and so on.

The sections to follow are intended to serve as a starting point for exploring your own style and the style of the people you work with from other countries. I suggest that you interpret this information in creative ways that relate to you and your company or organization. Ask yourself how the characteristics listed in each dimension relate to your particular situation. If you're on a work team that deals with other cultures, you might want to discuss these frameworks with your team members. For a hundred people, there will be a hundred different ways these issues apply. And the examples you come up with today may not apply in six months because situations and priorities change, so I also suggest you revisit this guide.

As was true with the five culture scales in Part 1, there will be an overlap of certain issues among the various themes in this section. For example, the first theme below, the role of managers, is separate from but can be related to the second theme, decision-making style, in that managers in flatter (less hierarchical) organizations might prefer a decision-making style that involves more employee input. As you read forward, you may find you build upon various dimensions or relate them to previous ones. While we can make some clear distinctions among certain issues when discussing cultures, I encourage you to recognize that not everything can be tightly compartmentalized and that there are naturally some overlaps and unexpected combinations that can be fascinating.

Try this approach: Read through the scales and see what strikes you as relevant. Maybe American workers with a German manager would read the first table, the "Role of Managers," and the word *formal* would jump off the page at them. They might think, "Oh yeah! Bucher (the German manager) is exactly like this—he does

Now go out there and think for yourselves!

it in a kind of half-joking way, but I really think he likes to use last names with the team. Even the way we have meetings seems to follow a stricter procedure than I'd use...I don't think just one person at a time should talk—I would rather have everyone toss out ideas. If I were running things, I think the atmosphere would be more relaxed."

Maybe you're reading this book independently, wanting help in understanding the international people who visit the health clinic you work in. Or maybe you will want to go through these tables as a starting point for discussions with the people you manage on your internationally mixed team. These issues apply to a variety of situations and settings where international cultures are part of the mix.

I have presented a few brief comments or examples after each table that may help get you started, but I don't want to lead you too much—you have to figure out how this relates to you. Circle numbers if you wish (for each nationality you interact with), and think of examples to justify your answer. Afterward, compare the numbers you circled with the numbers other members of your team circled and discuss any insights you have about differences in style.

The "Application" questions after each theme are intended to be a brief starting point that can lead to deeper discussion. These few specific questions are meant to get you started on examining these issues as they relate to your team or organization. These questions can also be useful for the individual in examining how he or she fits with a company culture. I suggest that you go through each Application question and commit a few answers to paper. When you've written your answers down, compare your insights with those of your colleagues. Hold one another accountable for well-considered answers if you're doing this as a team!

Management Issues

Role of Managers

	0	1	2	3	4	5	6	7	8	9	10	
"The Boss"	←										→	"Team Player"

• Hierarchy and clearly defined roles are expected.	• Equality and flexible roles rule the day.
• Decisions are dictated.	• Decision making is a shared process.
• Pyramid organization exists.	• Flat organization exists.

This scale applies the equality-hierarchy dimension to the role of managers. On the left of this scale, the boss (or manager, supervisor, etc.) makes all the decisions, and subordinates are expected to abide by them. The boss is being paid to make the decision and delegate responsibility to others to carry it out, and the subordinate is being paid to implement the boss' decision according to instructions.

In contrast, on the right side of the scale, the boss may decide what needs to get done, but the decision may be made with input from the employee and it's sometimes up to the employee to take responsibility for figuring out how to implement the decision.

Culture clash can happen when a boss from the right assumes that an employee from the left will solve a problem or make a decision him- or herself. In those instances, the boss gives minimal instruction and the employee frequently wanders off and does nothing while the team-player boss assumes things are being taken care of. They are not. The employee who is used to a stronger boss may be off thinking, "What is this manager trying to do, put her responsibility on me? Isn't she paid to make the decisions? It's not my job to figure out how things should be done; it's just my job to do what the boss tells me to." The result, of course, is that nothing gets done.

In the opposite case, a stronger boss from the left can be perceived as a micromanaging tyrant when a team-player employee is not allowed to make his or her own decisions or work out a way of implementing a directive.

Another difference here is that in flatter organizations the roles can be more flexible than in a pyramid organization. If you place a phone call to make a request in a hierarchical organization and the person who normally deals with those issues is unavailable, sometimes nothing will get done. You may have to wait until the person returns to the office for your request to be handled because it's not anyone else's job to take over. In a flatter organization there will be more flexibility, and other people can step in and take over the duties when their colleague is unavailable.

When dealing with their international colleagues, Americans, who may generally be accustomed to flatter organizations, are occasionally surprised that sometimes all they can do is wait until the proper person becomes available. "Can't *you* take care of this?" the American asks. The answer is often "No, that's Carmen's job and she returns on the fourteenth."

When dealing with hierarchies, it's crucial that you find the proper person to deal with. It's also important to follow the prescribed channels of communication. In at least some American organizations, you can go directly to the "Big Boss" with a problem, issue, or question. In many other countries, it's imperative that you go through the manager, then the director, and so on, up to the Big Boss. You will likely offend people if you "go over their heads" without consulting them.

Company culture can noticeably override country culture on this scale. For example, as I mentioned before, a military organization in *any* country will use a pyramidal style and all the levels of rank that go with it. You can sometimes gain insight into this aspect of your company's culture by looking at its roots. For example, some of the older airline companies still operating today were founded by former military men after World War II. Other, more recently formed airline companies have flatter organizational structures and correspondingly different management roles.

Application

1. How does your workplace rank on the above scale?

2. What specific practices lead you to think yours is a flatter or a more pyramidal organization?

3. How much of this is due to organizational culture and how much to country culture?

4. Have you experienced conflict or confusion at times of decision implementation or when instructions are given?

5. Do you notice differences in the roles and expectations of managers in any branch offices, especially overseas?

6. How could you redefine various work roles in your organization based on this information?

7. How could you personally benefit from redefining your own role as a manager with any subordinates?

8. Would it be beneficial if your superiors reconsidered their roles and allowed you to change yours? In what ways? How can you initiate this?

Decision-Making Style

0	1	2	3	4	5	6	7	8	9	10

⟵————————————————————————⟶

Consensus	Collaborative	Command

• After much talk, everyone agrees on a decision. • The decision is really an announcement of what has already been agreed upon over time.	• The leader collects input from everyone, then makes a decision.	• One person makes a decision and others are expected to abide by it.

Because Americans generally tend to be informal, their decision-making process can sometimes lean toward brainstorming and open discussions in which everyone is invited to offer their input or opinion, though the boss may still make the final decision. Such a style falls toward the center or the left of this scale.

Many others prefer a process with less brainstorming and fewer invitations for everyone to offer an opinion. In those scenarios, one person or a few key people make decisions, and the process resembles the center or the right of the scale.

As I suggested earlier, there is an echo here of elements from the five culture themes from Part 1. That is, the third culture scale ("Individual/Group") is relevant to this section in the following way: Group-focused cultures such as Japan are notorious for consensus-style decision making. But to confuse matters, the Japanese are also hierarchically focused (the first scale from Part 1, "Equality/Hierarchy"), and hierarchies lend themselves to command-style decisions.

This apparent confusion can be reconciled by considering that various decision styles are appropriate for various situations. If an urgent deadline is suddenly announced, a command style of decision making is probably best no matter what culture you're from. Instead of sitting around talking about long-range plans and building consensus, one person will say, "Mineko, make sure the warehouse knows about the raw material order! Tomo, call shipping and let them know we'll need 120 extra pallets in place by Tuesday!" and so forth.

So, depending on the decision to be made, the Japanese do indeed live up to their reputations as consensus decision makers but can also be command-style decision makers. I would point out here, as I similarly pointed out in my discussion of values and behaviors in Part 1, that we cannot *predict* how someone will make decisions based on what country he or she is from. We can, however, better understand why someone has made a particular decision in a particular way based on our knowledge of his or her culture, and we're sometimes able to anticipate possible or even likely (but never guaranteed) decision-making styles based on our knowledge of cultural styles.

To simplify things, I recommend that you know the various types of decision styles ranging from left to right on this scale and use them as a filter for explaining (and sometimes planning for) the decisions you may encounter in your international mixes. And more important, keep in mind that it's completely normal to encounter apparent contradictions and complexities on this theme (or any theme in Part 4).

The basic idea to remember is that clashes happen when you are expecting one decision-making style and your international partners or clients use another.

Application

1. Does your organization fit best toward the left, middle, or right of this scale (and how would you rank yourself on the scale)?

2. What types of decisions do you routinely make that involve consensus, collaborative, or command styles?

3. Are there ways in which the history of your organization or your field determines decision-making styles?

4. Does your organizational culture affect your decision-making style? If so, how?

5. Do you see ways in which your own national culture affects your decision-making style? If so, in what ways?

6. Do your international counterparts use a different style than you would in certain situations? If so, what situations?

7. How can you reconcile contradictory decision-making styles?

    a. Awareness of them is the first step. Who needs to be made aware of conflicting styles?

    b. Changing procedures or systems is a more significant step. How can you make this possible?

8. How can you change the flow of information to accommodate differences in decision-making styles between you and your international counterparts?

    a. What information could you provide or seek in different ways (e.g., e-mail through company channels) in order to improve the decision-making process?

    b. Could your decision-making process be improved by streamlining it or through greater involvement and information sharing?

Conflict Style

```
           0   1   2   3   4   5   6   7   8   9   10
Direct  ←─────────────────────────────────────────→  Indirect
```

• People say what they mean and mean what they say. • Conflict is good.	• It is important to be respectful and to maintain face and harmony. • Conflict is to be avoided.

This is a typical area of conflict between East and West. In the West, we ideally say what we mean and mean what we say. When an American tells you that a shipment can be sent by Tuesday, he or she almost certainly means that the shipment will be shipped when promised. If it isn't shipped Tuesday, the company's or individual's reputation is tarnished. When Americans or Canadians mean yes they will usually say yes; likewise, no means no. On the other hand, the Chinese and Japanese are especially known for saying yes when they mean maybe, maybe when they mean no, and "It's difficult" (or even yes) when they actually mean no. This represents indirectness, not dishonesty.

Having a direct or indirect conflict style also determines which issues will be discussed and which will be avoided. Those with a direct conflict style may be very willing to "get issues out on the table," whereas indirect communicators may prefer to say nothing about sensitive topics rather than say the wrong thing. Or they may prefer to delay discussions and wait until more information is available, more time has passed, more decisions have been made, and so forth.

Application

1. How would you rank yourself on this scale? Do you consider yourself a diplomatic person?

2. Are there situations when your international counterparts are more (direct or indirect) than you expect? If yes, in what situations?

3. If you are more (direct or indirect) than usual with your international counterparts to match their style, how might this be an

advantage? (Or should they change their style to match yours? If so, how and why?)

4. Is your ranking on this scale influenced by the nature of your job or by the atmosphere within your your company? That is, do you have to be more (direct or indirect) at work than you might normally be? If so, are there ways in which your own natural "outside-of-work" style might be more effective?

5. Are there work situations where you would need or prefer to be indirect? Are there issues you won't or cannot discuss openly? What are those situations or issues?

Work Style

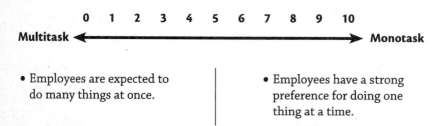

- Employees are expected to do many things at once.

- Employees have a strong preference for doing one thing at a time.

Almost all of my workshop participants think they multitask when I present this concept to them, because almost everyone feels over-worked and must indeed do many things at once. But here's a clue that will show the style of your country: watch how people wait in line—do they mob around a cashier or do they proceed one at a time? The British are known for "queuing up." Many South Americans, Middle Easterners, and Asians crowd around the cashier, all seeking attention at the same time. There are no laws in Britain that people have to wait in line, they simply do so; this behavior indicates British cultural pro-gramming. As an American, I have similar programming. Frequently, when I go to the deli counter in the United States, I take a number and wait until it is called, or when I go to the bank, I wait in one long line for my turn. I even *prefer* to do this! It ensures that there is no skip-ping ahead in line; I feel secure that I will be served when it's my turn. Furthermore, the clerk behind the counter will not be required to mul-titask by helping three people at once.

This preference for working on one task or multiple tasks simultaneously also affects office behavior. Based on my cultural programing, most times I don't like it when someone takes a phone call (business or personal) during a meeting with me. But in some cultures, people may have conversations with several visitors at once. There is no need to be offended if they talk on the phone while you are in their office or if they invite one or more others who stop by to join the meeting. It may even be to your advantage—one of those visitors might prove to be a valuable contact!

Application

1. Again, everyone thinks they multitask. But what does your job actually require of you? (Where does your work environment rank on the scale?)

2. Left to your own devices (outside a work setting), where would you rank on this scale?

3. How do your international counterparts rank differently from you, and what conflicts or difficulties does this create?

4. How could you reconcile any such conflicts or difficulties? Is there a system or procedure that could be put in place to accommodate or minimize these differences?

Employee Motivation and Rewards

| 0 | 1 | 2 | 3 | 4 | 5 | 6 | 7 | 8 | 9 | 10 |

Personal ←――――――――――――――――――――→ Impersonal

- Personal or customized rewards, such as a gift certificate or recognition
- Intrinsic motivation

- Impersonal or standardized rewards, such as cash
- Extrinsic motivation

How should employees be motivated toward good performance? Some will be delighted to receive a T-shirt or a plaque on the wall as a team performance reward. One French person told me that a T-shirt with words across the chest (offered as a team performance reward from his American parent company) might as well say *"Hello! I'm an idiot!"* The French sometimes want cash rewards in situations where Americans would be satisfied with a gift or a dinner certificate. An American supervisor confided to me, "If I recognize an [American] employee with a gift certificate for a $100 dinner, it will have a lot more impact than a $100 bonus. The $100 bonus is almost an insult—it barely adds anything to the monthly salary, but he or she will remember the classy dinner!"

Discussions of employee motivation can center on phrases like "intrinsic motivation" (motivation based on the desire for pleasure or satisfaction of performing a job well) and "extrinsic rewards" (e.g., motivation based on a cash bonus received for good performance). It is commonly thought that if employees focus too much on the extrinsic reward, they lose their intrinsic motivation for performing the task. These employees might say of their jobs, "I'm only in it for the money."

I suggest that these concepts can help us understand two difficulties with motivation and rewards in international mixes. First, we don't always know what extrinsic reward to give. Common sense says that if you give the wrong reward (the T-shirt to the Frenchman when he was expecting cash), the employee will definitely lose motivation. Second, we don't know what kind of intrinsic motivation is operating in the heads of our international employees (e.g., what makes a Spaniard love her job?). What brings job satisfaction to a Russian may not bring job satisfaction to a Filipino.

So, in very plain English: Don't assume that the rewards you give effectively in your culture will motivate people from all cultures. Reward systems vary around the world in every culture, company, and situation, as does motivation. Find out how managers from the local culture motivate their employees by asking the employees. And perhaps the best way (though not the easiest) to learn what motivates an employee is to get to know that person. For example, as you get to know your Filipino employees, find out what they like, what motivates them intrinsically, and how they might prefer to be rewarded extrinsically. There's no magic answer for what reward will motivate Filipinos, but the better you know them, the better you will be at identifying a special way to recognize their good performance.

Application

1. What increases your intrinsic motivation in your job?

2. Can you recognize ways in which your international employees' intrinsic motivations might differ from yours? (This is not a question I expect anyone to be able to answer quickly. It's more of a suggested research project for you.)

3. What are small (or large) ways you motivate or reward employees?

4. Who are some people who might not be motivated by your choices because of cultural background?

5. Can you name situations where you might need to change your practices for giving rewards?

6. How might you need to change to accommodate these people and situations?

Work Priorities

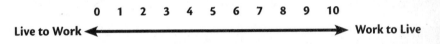

Americans sometimes complain, "I work 60 or 70 hours a week." Sometimes such complaining almost sounds like boasting! To those from cultures where people work to live, a 60-hour workweek would be nothing to boast about! Maybe I can start a trend by being the first working American to boast I'm working 30 to 40 hours a week. Actually, I'd like to get it down to 15 to 20 hours.

Not everyone values work to the same degree. Scandinavians, for example, are known for leaving the office at 5:00 P.M. and not looking back. Around the world people are amazed that many Americans tolerate a mere two weeks of vacation per year. As I mentioned in Part 1, some countries offer starting employees more generous vacations than Americans are given in their final work years. The lesson? Don't expect your international co-workers to keep the same weekly work hours as you do—or to be satisfied with a mere two weeks of vacation per year.

Americans relocate around the United States often and willingly. People from most other countries are amazed that Americans appear ready to sacrifice anything for work—such as uprooting and relocating their families frequently, apparently placing work before family, friends, leisure time, and even their own health.

For most people in most countries, work is a part of life, not life itself. And those countries seem to survive just fine. The grocery stores are stocked with food, the economies are indeed robust, and all this in spite of the fact that the population is not work crazed.

Application

1. How do you rank yourself on this scale?

   a. Do you work evenings and weekends?

   b. How much vacation time have you become accustomed to receiving over your career?

   c. How much vacation are your international colleagues accustomed to receiving?

2. Do you respond with what you do when someone asks who you are? Has your job title become your primary way of identifying yourself? How might you define yourself outside of work and outside your job title?

3. How do you rank your international counterparts on this scale? (Give examples.)

4. Have differences in priorities about work led to any conflicts within your organization?

5. The nature of any industry or job requires a commitment to a certain set of work values. That said, how could you benefit from changing your emphasis in this area? Should others change? If so, how and why?

Strategy Issues

There are myriad issues you must consider when bringing a product to market internationally or when selling a product to specific international groups in your own country. Cultural differences affect how people respond to advertising and marketing approaches, and they dictate your decisions about product pricing and quality. Issues such as shopping habits and consumer behaviors vary worldwide and need to be taken into consideration from the moment you design your product or service to the point of sale.

For example, consider the fact that Europeans have smaller kitchen appliances (stoves, refrigerators, microwaves) than Americans do. It makes sense, then, that many Europeans shop daily for food and purchase it in small quantities. Contrast this with the American practice in many households of going to the supermarket once a week or even once every two weeks. Americans can do this, given their large vehicles, enormous refrigerators, cupboard space, and sometimes extra freezers for storage of food. And tastes differ among nations. For example, the Japanese don't have as much fat in their diets as Americans do; their vice is perhaps salty foods. Country to country, noon or evening meals vary in length, meaning, and preferred menu. Is alcohol typically served with a businessperson's lunch? And is that lunch two hours long or just thirty minutes? All these aspects and others would need to be considered by an American food company planning to introduce a line overseas. What is successful domestically will not automatically catch on overseas.

In addition to how you design a product, how you sell it differs globally. Consider for a moment what will convince you to buy a product. What will keep your attention long enough to read or listen to the end of an ad? In the United States, ads are often direct, short, and to the point. If an American woman is buying a handbag, for example, she might be impressed to read that the bag is (1) waterproof, (2) durable, and (3) reasonably priced.

I saw a French ad for leather bags that began something like this:

> *In life we always notice imperfections first. Imagine the effect that can have when one looks at a beautiful woman....*

The ad went on (rather interminably in my opinion) to describe the harmony of the stitching process, how each handmade leather bag from this company has flaws that enhance its uniqueness, and so forth. This looked like some kind of prose, not an advertisement. Americans don't usually have patience for ads like this.

There are entire textbooks written on international sales, advertising, marketing, product design, brand management, and so forth. My hope in the next few sections is to get you thinking about a few issues regarding strategy; whether you sell a product or a service, I want to encourage you to consider how you might modify your approach to fit the various cultures you interact with. Topics will include views on change, level of control over life, and the meaning of quality. To get started, you can apply my comments in this section (and the Application questions below) in a variety of ways; these issues are relevant to companies selling widgets overseas as well as to companies serving international populations domestically.

Application

1. To what cultural groups do you market your products and/or services?

2. In what ways have you already successfully changed your marketing/advertising approaches for these groups?

3. In what ways do you see that you may have missed opportunities to change your marketing/advertising approaches for these groups?

4. How might you need to change your marketing approach to better tap into these groups?

5. Are there people from those cultures who are readily available for giving you critical feedback and insights about your current marketing approaches? Are you taking advantage of these resources? If not, how could you?

6. Might you need to go deeper than marketing and advertising and actually change the product itself or the way you deliver the service in order to be successful?

Views on Change

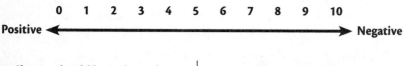

| 0 | 1 | 2 | 3 | 4 | 5 | 6 | 7 | 8 | 9 | 10 |

Positive ←————————————————————————→ Negative

- Change should be embraced and encouraged.

- Change should be approached cautiously.

Are you comfortable with change or threatened by it? Openness to change and tolerance of the accompanying risks go hand in hand. As I mentioned in Part 1 in the discussion of the risk/caution scale, American companies make very bold statements about change and risk and embracing the new. Professionals from other countries often feel threatened by change because of the risk it involves.

One client from an American manufacturing company reported the following about the Japanese: "Every change I communicate to them is met with many questions. They want to know the 'why' for every single decision. Every little change causes a delay that must be planned for." Part of my recommendation for that client was to establish an online policy manual accessible to its Japanese distributors. Each term, policy, rule, preference, practice, and so forth (e.g., shipping practices, paperwork needed for completing orders, payment deadlines, and discount schedules) were written out and numbered. The Japanese counterparts loved this document. When changes occurred (due to inconsistencies or oversights), the Japanese would refer back to the document: "But it says in number 17 of the shipping guide that customs documents need to be...." This helped the American company identify inconsistencies and avoid unnecessary and confusing changes in procedure, and it provided a stable reference point and procedural guide to the Japanese.

Application

1. Is your industry or field constantly experiencing change or is it rather stable?

2. How does your company rank on the above scale? Are changes continual? Are they necessary? How would you rank your personal preference?

3. Which changes are truly unavoidable? Which are avoidable? Which are desirable?

4. How do your international counterparts rank on this scale?

5. Have differences in style caused conflicts?

6. How could you benefit by adjusting your style in this area? For example, could you portray yourself as less change oriented if your international counterparts were not comfortable with certain changes?

7. What systems could you put into place to help minimize the negative effects of unavoidable changes?

Level of Control over Life and Business

```
       0   1   2   3   4   5   6   7   8   9   10
In Control ◄──────────────────────────────────► Not in Control
```

• We are in control of our fate.	• Our fate controls us; we must accept it.

Almost every year there are devastating floods in various parts of the globe. Generally, in Western countries there is little or no loss of life in spite of the tremendous property damage. Sadly, in less developed areas (South Asia, for example), thousands of people often die in mudslides and from drowning, their homes and animals washed away.

Why does flooding result in so many human casualties in one place and not another? Is the flooding that much worse in some areas? Yes, geography (areas with monsoons and hurricane-prone countries), development, and infrastructure are certainly factors. But another explanation is that Western countries believe in taking control (even of Mother Nature!). Westerners track the precipitation all year and prepare well in advance of the flood. Crews put sandbags out and populations are evacuated. People in some non-Western cultures seem more likely to accept losses and even death as their fate and are less likely to think they can do anything to protect themselves from nature's cruelties. For many, unfortunately, when the floods come, people die.

Whether people believe they are in control of their own lives or feel that they are controlled by external circumstances or nature or a god, beliefs in this area certainly affect the way people work, plan, do business, and get through life. These beliefs affect specific tasks, such as how people manage projects, or general values, such as how much importance they place on working hard to better themselves.

Application

1. Do you believe you are in control of your life? Your business?

2. Do your international counterparts believe they are in control of their lives? Their business?

3. Which mistake do you think would be better to make, a or b:

   a. to believe you are in control of your life when you really might not be?

   b. to believe you are not in control of your life when you really might be?

4. What are the benefits of being in control of life and business?

5. What are the benefits of "going with the flow" and letting go of some control?

6. Does your industry require exercising a high or a low level of control? (Engineers don't leave much up to fate when a machine is out of spec; they take control and fix it. Weather forecasters can't control the weather; they must respond to it.)

7. Can you identify ways in which changing your style on this scale would benefit your international counterparts? Might they need to change to be more compatible with you or with the demands of your industry? How?

Quality

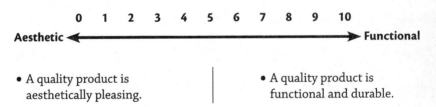

What is quality to a Frenchman is not necessarily quality to a German. How do you define quality? For example, what is a quality VCR? For me, it might cost $100 to $200 (I assume a $35 VCR would be junk), and it should last at least five or six years. If it breaks in two years, I'll know I "got taken," but I don't expect it to last twenty years either. For a German, a quality item is expected to last a lifetime. Germans are sometimes not interested in service contracts because the item should never malfunction in the first place. To a French person, a quality item should be pleasing to look at, and to a Swede it should be designed artistically. Many Americans think anything plastic is of poor quality. A Chinese person, on the other hand, may not care if an item is made of plastic as long as it *looks* good. ISO* certification may be an objective indicator that a company offers quality products, but there are no guidelines accepted by every culture for what quality means, because the concept is subjective.

In addition to considering the culture you are dealing with, pay attention to the specific industry. Even within a country, quality in the automobile industry is defined differently from quality in consulting or in the small consumer goods sector.

Consider this: What did "Made in Japan" mean fifty years ago? People generally respond that it meant junk. Now it generally means high quality. The Japanese inspire American manufacturers with everything from their high-quality electronics to automobiles. Does the phrase "Made in China" imply high quality today? I think most would say it doesn't, but that, too, may change. What does the phrase "Made in the USA" mean in your industry? Americans do make good products, but you're not likely to impress a German by boasting that you offer "Made-in-the-USA quality."

Application

1. How do you define quality in your products or services? Do you have objective standards for measuring it? Do you have any established subjective quality guidelines?

2. Do you see ways in which your international counterparts may not be pleased with the current quality of your products or services? (Describe these.)

3. What improvements in your products or services could you possibly make based on these quality issues?

4. Should you be expected to live up to the quality standards of your international customers? Can you afford to offer lower quality than they expect?

---

* ISO stands for the International Organization for Standardization, which promotes quality and environmental standards.

Planning Style

Ready, Aim, Fire

With the "ready, aim, fire" style of planning, decisions can take a long time in the making, but once all the deciding and planning are done, the results can be implemented quickly. Japan, Germany, and Sweden are examples where this is often the case.

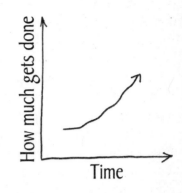

Planners from most cultures prefer to look, and look carefully, before they leap, taking plenty of time in the process. Look at the graph. Not much is achieved in the beginning, but as time goes on, things do happen, and happen quickly! What can sometimes seem like a frustratingly slow start to Americans can actually result in a longer-term payoff.

Ready, Fire, Aim

Americans take note: We in the United States seem to be more comfortable than anyone else with fast-paced change based on quickly made plans. We are often frustrated by the slow and deliberate planning processes of our international partners. Our style is to spend as little time as possible in the planning phase of a project and then jump into implementing it, where prog-

ress often seems to get bogged down. This is part of the explanation of why many American companies will send expatriates overseas without any cross-cultural or language training. We grab for the fast market share, and we believe that the early bird gets the worm. Imagine how threatening the uncertainty of this fast-paced approach can be to those who deal with Americans.

Recall the letter at the end of Part 1 from the Dutchman who actually wrote "Ready-Fire-Aim." Not all planning styles are so overtly announced. Many are shocked at how quickly Americans want to proceed without having made careful plans. General advice to American companies and individuals is to be careful not to push their international partners too quickly with the American ready-fire-aim approach.

Planning also relates to the way we make day-to-day decisions and how carefully we prepare for smaller initiatives, but this also may be a good time for me to touch on planning in the bigger, strategic sense. As I mentioned above, American companies are not known for preparing employees well for international assignments.

Recall the manager from "XYZ Company" I referred to in Part 2 who was sent to Tokyo for several years without any cross-cultural training. This is not atypical. In my experience, only rarely do companies offer any training or deliberate preparation for employees going overseas for short or even long assignments. And, unbelievably, sometimes the only preparation for someone going to Thailand on a business assignment is to take him out for a Thai meal or to arrange a conversation with someone who has been to Thailand or who is from Thailand. Of course, being from Thailand (or any country) does not make you an expert on that country. I am amazed to see otherwise savvy companies that are domestically successful and sometimes globally successful send employees overseas almost totally unprepared. If companies are already successful globally, the rationale seems to go, why should they train their employees? My answer is that just because a company has achieved global success does not mean every employee of that company will be successful internationally or is beyond needing cross-cultural strategy and training.

A major company with hundreds of millions (or billions) in revenue may be able to absorb a hundred-thousand-dollar loss as a result of sending an employee overseas without preparation. Smaller companies cannot, and in my experience, smaller companies are often the ones that plan more carefully. Even if a company is successful as a global player, individual employees need help dealing with the day-to-day challenges inherent

> **Strategic planning for international initiatives still needs to be done at the individual level even when there is great global success at the company level.**

in international ventures: languages, currencies, banking systems, accounting practices, legal systems, transportation structures, political systems, human resources systems, product labeling laws, and so forth. All of these differences mean uncertainty and thus the need for careful planning from the broader strategic level down to the individual support level.

Application

1. Which model describes the style of your international colleagues? (Again, give examples.)

2. Which model best describes your planning style? (Give examples.)

3. How have these planning-style differences led to clashes in past projects?

4. How can clashes or frustrations be avoided in the future? (Focus especially on what you can do to make things smoother; it's easier to make changes in yourself than in others.)

People and Communication Issues

Freedom versus Identity

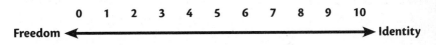

0	1	2	3	4	5	6	7	8	9	10	

Freedom ◄───────────────────────────────► Identity

• People should be free to be whoever they want to be—the sky's the limit.	• People should know clearly who they are and accept their position or role in life.

Freedom and identity are not polar opposites like the headings of most of the other scales I present, but they still represent two sides of a coin, and the contrast they present can offer important insights into the cultural programming of the world's people. This issue relates most readily to the discussion of the role of women in different cultures.

Are there female construction workers in your culture? How about female CEOs? Male nurses? Male secretaries? They may not exist in great numbers, but is role flexibility even possible? Both women and men are gradually taking on roles that were formerly limited to the other sex in the United States because of the American emphasis on equality. Yes, I acknowledge that women encounter glass ceilings and inequities in the U.S. workplace and society, but my point is that many American women are proud of being able to handle their own finances, of excelling in their careers, of changing their own tires, and of being independent.

In some other parts of the world there are no female CEOs, no male nurses, and so forth. When most South American couples go out together in a car, for example, it is usually the man who drives. This can leave American women uncomfortable, but other interpretations are also possible. In the context of a discussion on this topic with my MBA students, a woman from Ghana told me, "I would much rather be *driven* than drive my own car."

On another subject, are Muslim women *forced* to wear veils, according to many Westerners, or do they choose to wear them? Muslims (many women included) will point out that women *prefer* to wear veils because it is a positive part of their religious and social identity. They enjoy their role as honor bearers of the family.

Americans tend to think that women who do not drive or women who wear a veil are somehow oppressed and will "see the light" once they learn a little bit more about Western gender equality. Such perspectives are important to understand as more Westerners come face-to-face with Muslims.

When I ask (just to spark a little conversation), "What about women who are not *allowed* to drive?" the discussion usually turns to whether these women really want to drive. It is usually the Americans in the class who will eventually guide this kind of debate to the position that *freedom to choose* is the most important thing. But this concept of personal freedom is a Western cultural tenet. Americans in particular are proud of how much freedom we have in the United States, and we boast about the choices we have. But I would encourage the reader to question whether the choices between Pepsi and Coke, K-mart and Target, McDonald's and Burger King, Ford and Chevy are really significantly distinct choices. There is hardly any difference between the American Democratic and Republican Parties when you consider them alongside those of the French, which range from the extremely right-wing National Front Party to the leftist Communist Party. Such variety also exists in many other countries.

Although Americans enjoy freedom of the press and freedom of movement, visitors to the United States sometimes point out that we accept heavier limits on our freedom than we realize. Lewis Lapham writes this critical thought of Americans and their freedoms:

> *In place of the reckless and independent-minded individual once thought to embody the national stereotype (child of nature, descendant of Daniel Boone, hard-drinking and unorthodox), we now have a quorum of nervous careerists, psalm-singing and well-behaved, happy to oblige, eager to please, trained to hold up their hands and empty their pockets when passing through airport security or entering City Hall. (2003, 8)*[†]

Indeed more Americans are becoming upset with shocking new government initiatives that threaten even constitutionally guaranteed freedoms.

As the dialogue goes back and forth in this way, the issues boil down to freedom to choose (valued by Americans) versus a clearly defined identity (valued by many others). Although Americans might not be comfortable with mere acceptance of one's place in society, such acceptance of one's proper role is perfectly okay and makes sense within other cultures.

It is not my intention to bring this into a deep debate about ethics or to raise issues about human rights. I only want to identify the freedom versus identity continuum because it affects our international working relationships. What we expect of the men and women who are our international counterparts may not be what they are accustomed to or are comfortable with.

Application

1. How do you rank yourself on this scale? (Give some examples and reasons why.)

2. How do you rank your international partners or customers on this scale? (Again, explain.)

[†] *Harper's* Magazine, February 2003 (Published by Harper's Magazine Foundation, New York, New York).

3. Have you ever perceived your male international counterparts as "sexist" or the women as "weak"? How much of this is due to your own cultural programming?

4. What changes might you want to make in the way you deal with people, based on this issue?

Pace of Life

0	1	2	3	4	5	6	7	8	9	10

Time as Scarce   **Time as Plentiful**

- Move quickly—time is a limited resource.
- Move slowly—time is an abundant resource.

This category will play out in many ways according to the situation. The simple idea here is that many people outside the United States proceed much more slowly than Americans do. This often irritates Americans, who don't expect or understand it. A typical scenario is the American who "pops overseas" for a few days of meetings. He or she can feel impatient, then frustrated, when the host counterparts do not get straight to business.

Americans view time as valuable, a scarce resource. We attach the language of money to time: we spend it, save it, waste it, and budget it. We use calendar software to monitor, coordinate, and fill our schedules much like we use financial software to track our checkbooks.

"Time is money!" Why waste a business trip just touring around!?

Others are more relaxed about time. This is to be expected with older cultures; if dozens of generations have passed in the centuries before you, it's natural to take a more relaxed view of time. If something doesn't get accomplished today, there is always tomorrow.

The clash happens when Americans think that in order to have a successful trip they should accomplish something—such as negotiating a firm agreement. Others will feel that a business trip is successful just because they met and got to know their colleagues. Business can and will happen later...over time. Americans can go bonkers if they invested the time and money to fly across an ocean and "serious business" was not discussed or a deal closed. It's sometimes hard for Americans to realize how pointless it is to press for a deadline when dealing with someone whose culture has survived quite well without deadlines (and certainly without American products) for thousands of years.

People who live under time pressures tend to want to accomplish a task before it's too late (whatever "too late" means—with an infinite future in front of you, how can anything be too late?). It so happens that others who do not feel time pressures as much prefer to focus on building proper business relationships, which is naturally expected to take some time.

Application

1. How do you rank yourself and your partners on this scale? Are there specific instances where conflicting views on time have come into play?

2. What are some areas where you absolutely cannot afford to slow your pace of business?

3. How could you benefit by changing your business sense of time and pace (either faster or slower)? Should others change? How and why?

4. How might you improve business in the long run by changing (yes, even slowing) your pace of business and considering time as abundant?

Courtesy, Protocol, Formality

	0	1	2	3	4	5	6	7	8	9	10	

Informal ←————————————————————————→ Formal

• Courtesies and protocols are largely unnecessary—relax and be yourself.	• Courtesies and protocols are important—be considerate of others.

Entire books have been written on the protocols to be followed in many specific countries. There are also guidebooks on how to behave during specific functions, for example, a Chinese business dinner. The recommendation I make in this section is a general one and it is offered primarily to Americans. *Pay attention to the numerous ways your international colleagues are more formal than you are.* Notice the little protocols they respect, the small courtesies they engage in. These things may seem trivial, but they are important. Below are a few examples.

Outward appearances *do* count. Americans can be found wearing sweat pants or jogging shorts to the grocery store. We could argue that this is fine in that it shows how informal Americans are. I could agree with that. What does it matter, after all, if you wear a dumpy sweatshirt when you're only dropping by the store for a minute? Society won't screech to a halt. But in fact it matters a lot to many non-Americans, who wouldn't be caught dead wearing their exercise clothing outside of an exercise environment. You don't wear gym clothes to a store any more than you would wear a three-piece suit to a beach. This is something I can agree with too!

While my American friends come to a party wearing jeans, tennis shoes, and T-shirts, my South American and European friends wear pressed pants, leather shoes, nice dresses, and button-down shirts. Whether you're entertaining international visitors or engaging in business on their home turf, I encourage you to pay attention to and follow the local dress codes. If you want to be casual at home, go for it. Just be aware that you may be perceived in other places or by visitors from other countries as poorly raised.

Other behaviors count as well: Americans put their feet up on train benches, relax and slouch back in their chairs at meetings, and comfortably call one another by first names. This casual approach is not valued universally. I recommend that in addition to paying attention to clothing, you watch how people generally carry themselves and treat others. Do they engage in behaviors of courtesy that you might consider unnecessary, such as politely opening doors for a client or pouring tea for her? Notice how others greet. To Americans the initial greeting doesn't matter too much, but to many, men are expected to shake hands and women to kiss each other on both cheeks the first time they see each other on a given day. I witnessed one instance when a French friend was holding an armload of books, so he apologized and offered his elbow for a colleague to shake when he saw him for the first time that day. Not doing so would have been the equivalent of snubbing the other person. Again, watch what the locals do and emulate it appropriately if possible.

In addition to the way you present yourself through dress or physical behavior, objects can indicate your degree of formality. As a professor I have noticed that when many of my international students submit a paper to me, the presentation of the paper—how it is bound, how crisp the pages are—seems to count almost as much to them as the content of the paper itself. An American professor may tolerate dog-eared pages if the thoughts are good and the essential information is present; others will not.

Language is another area where Americans have an opportunity to either do well or bumble with formality and courtesy. English does not make distinctions between formal and informal ways of saying *you,* as many other languages do. For example, the French use *vous* for the formal "you" (between new acquaintances, or to show respect) and *tu* for the informal "you" (as between friends). The same is true in many languages such as German, Spanish, Italian, Portuguese, Swedish, Norwegian, and so on. Even if you are not actually speaking the foreign language, be aware that the native speakers of that language *do* make distinctions between formal and informal, and it is important that you address people you don't know very well with respect, even in English.

Almost everywhere else in the world, Americans must expect more attention to courtesy, formality, and protocol in ways like those mentioned above. When Americans find themselves thinking, "Do we really need to go through all this hassle?" the answer is usually a resounding "Yes!" Pay careful attention to the protocols of others and imitate them when you can and in ways you think are appropriate.

Application

1. Do you lean toward the formal or informal side of this scale?

2. What examples of courtesy, formality, or protocol have you already seen in your international partners? Are there specific behaviors or ways of speaking or dressing that come to mind?

3. What might your international colleagues' impressions of you be? Would they be positive or negative?

4. Do you believe these things are really important? If so, how can you avoid clashes and present yourself more successfully by changing your placement on this scale?

Reasoning Styles

If you are a scientist conducting precise chemical experiments or a designer sketching out a basic marketing storyboard, of course your job will require you to think within a fairly restricted cognitive style. Below I am not describing such specified logic systems. My hope is to describe general thinking styles and suggest that they may vary across cultures.

Of course this is an area where individual differences in thinking and processing information will play a huge role—much of the time overshadowing cultural differences. Still, this will be a useful guide to help you understand the people you deal with from other cultures. You may say, "Ah! *That's* why Italian advertising is done that way!"

Start with the Conclusion

One approach is to start with a conclusion or hypothesis or statement and then find a way to back it up with points. We spiral our way out from the conclusion. As long as the points along the way all support our initial hypothesis and do not contradict one another, we feel we can support our conclusion.

Here's an example: I might start with the statement, "Human cloning *should not* be done." I might support that conclusion by citing religious reasons or by saying that experimenting with human lives in this way is unethical or by using the argument that in the wrong hands, cloning technology could be used to dangerous ends. As long as all of my points somehow support my hypothesis that human cloning is wrong and don't contradict one another, I will feel confident that my conclusion can be taken as correct.

Or, I can take the opposite view. I start by concluding, "Human cloning *should* be advanced." I cite reasons such as these: human cloning will advance medical understanding and save lives, science must continually move forward, and so on. As long as all my statements support my beginning conclusion and don't contradict one another, I can make a strong argument for human cloning.

This thinking style can be called "inductive" thinking. It permits extreme opposite views (with their supporting evidence) to exist side by side. In fact, induction is the kind of reasoning that people use to support opposite views on tough issues such as abortion, the death penalty, or racial bias. We can see such conflicting perspectives clashing in American society in dramatic ways. Freedom of speech and of the press allow these clashes to be debated in the open and are perhaps part of the explanation for why many from other cultures see Americans as extremists on issues such as gun ownership, gender, and other ideas that we have the freedom to voice our differences about.

Finish with the Conclusion

Another approach is to collect data, consult experts, run studies, and then arrive at a conclusion. Using this approach, you work your way inward and won't know for certain what your conclusion will be until you arrive at it.

If we were to use this style to investigate a research issue, we would strive to start without making any conclusions. We would instead begin by asking questions, reviewing the literature, collecting facts, and then seeing where all our research, questioning, logic, reasoning, and philosophizing take us.

Again, I'm not describing formal logic systems here, but this thinking style looks pretty similar to the French philosopher Descartes' "deductive" reasoning. This is the approach that scientific researchers are supposed to take; instead of starting with a conclusion, they are expected to start with an open mind and let the data tell what they will.

I'm going to go way out on a limb (for just a moment) to tentatively suggest that this might indeed be a French way of thinking, and maybe a European way in general. This kind of cognitive style may have spread with the Spanish and Portuguese to South America as well. It may be that their school systems emphasize this kind of thinking, and that certainly has an impact in later years. Graduate students in many research-focused fields are certainly groomed to think this way. Certain professions may naturally groom their members to think this way. Researchers, for example, should have no preconceptions about what results they might find; they go about collecting data, and whatever conclusions emerge are supposed to be beyond their control. (Far too often, though, that isn't what really happens.)

It would be a gross overgeneralization to say that people from any given country or field think this way in all situations (I'm back off my limb now). I want to emphasize again that of course one can't define a thinking style that accurately describes all people from a country. Also, every task, issue, situation, and question can be different and may therefore require a particular reasoning style.

The point is that once we identify a few different reasoning styles, we might begin to better understand how important thinking styles are when we mix, manage, plan, and make decisions with people from various cultures.

Arrive at the Conclusion All at Once

This third style is less linear than the two previous approaches. The first two styles followed a path of reasoning: outward *from* a conclusion or inward *toward* one. With this third thinking style, the conclusion is more or less "arrived at all at once," based on the consideration of many things from many directions or categories. If  you're arriving at a conclusion all at once and from many directions, you can't really get there by following a straight path.

A debate process where people take opposite sides might not work well with this reasoning style. I recall a discussion our class had in an early grad school class; the professor asked if teaching was an art or a science. We were supposed to go around the class offering opinions. The first person said teaching was a science in that one could follow certain principles of learning and teaching, but at the same time teaching was an art in that it required talent or feeling on the teacher's part to be able to really connect with students. As the professor called on each of us around the circle, we all basically gave some variation on that answer. When it came to the Japanese student, however, he told us he didn't see why art and science should be contradictory positions. He proposed that they were different aspects of the same idea. This was the first really different answer presented by anyone in the class.

This third reasoning style could well be considered an Asian or Middle Eastern style. It could be called "holistic" thinking. This style lends itself to consensus building, which is a typically Asian practice. In Asian consensus building, everyone offers input; facts, hypotheses, and opinions are collected and exchanged.

This way of thinking can be a rather slow process, so when I say a conclusion is arrived at all at once, I don't mean that it happens overnight. It might be arrived at "suddenly" after several months of reflection and discussion.

Application

1. Which of these three styles do you use most? (Give some examples.)

2. Do you think your style is determined by your field, your culture, your personality, or a combination of these? (Give examples.)

3. How do your international partners prefer to think and reason? (Again, give examples.)

4. Are there incompatibilities that arise because of differences in your and your international partners' reasoning styles?

5. How could you benefit by modifying your own thinking and reasoning style? Should others change also? How and why?

Cognitive Style and Communication

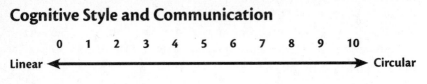

0	1	2	3	4	5	6	7	8	9	10

Linear ⬅————————————————➡ Circular

- Linear thinking moves in a straight line to the point, without getting sidetracked.

- Circular or systemic thinking is tangential, looping and looping closer to the point.

Linear thinking goes straight to the point whereas by *circular* thinking I mean that the speaker might loop several times on tangents but eventually will return to the point. Just about any time you hear these two terms, *linear* and *circular*, they are used critically; we accuse people of circular thinking if they use faulty, repetitive logic, and we accuse them of linear thinking when we really mean narrow thinking. The point I wish to make about international communication with these two styles is a simple one and is not intended as critical in any way.

This is yet one more instance when we must remember that there are many exceptions to any "rule" we come up with, because individual differences will outweigh any supposed cultural trends. With those disclaimers, what follows is some plain-English discussion on how the way we think affects the way we communicate.

How do you convey your thoughts to others? How do you make the bridge from knowing what's in your head to expressing it so that another person can understand it? What approach do you use during presentations, discussions, negotiations, or conversations with clients, customers, partners, or employees?

Straight to the Point

In the United States, it is perfectly acceptable, preferable, and in fact expected for a person to go straight to the point.

Americans tend to follow a predictable sequence. They often go from point A to point F with a predictable passage through points B, C, D, and E. They don't want to get sidetracked. Americans like to organize their thoughts in this linear fashion so that they can accomplish their objectives in short order.

How strongly Americans behave this way depends of course on the situation overall—and on the personality. In some instances, they may indeed stray from their straight-arrow course and in fact loop around the point, but we can say that Americans generally value clear and linear organization.

Here's the U.S. style:

Your brain   *The point*

Meander to the Point

This is the style of many people from around the world. Because of their focus on harmony and indirect communication, Japanese speakers (among other Asians) sometimes prefer to circle around the point when getting straight to it might appear blunt.

Some speakers who have particularly relaxed views on time, notably Arabs, Russians, and Africans, might seem to meander to the point, inserting stories and tangents. They may then circle around it with an anecdote or three. Their path may zig-zag and become sidetracked, but eventually they *do* get to the point.

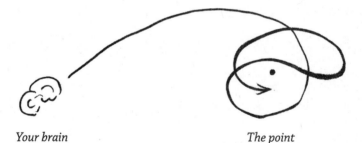

Your brain   *The point*

When the two styles mix, obviously there can be clashes. People of either style will frustrate and confuse people of the other style: Americans can be frustrated by all the tangents and "wasted time" when talking with international colleagues, wondering what the point of the conversation or meeting is. And many others feel put off or feel insulted by Americans, who appear to them to be "pushy" and incapable of appreciating subtlety. The "meanderers'" tangents and loops lead them gradually to the point without insulting their audience's intelligence by pounding their point into the listener's head.

Each way of communicating does indeed eventually get to the point (or very close to it). So patience is always recommended!

Application

1. Which reasoning style or styles do you and your international associates use? (Can you find examples of how either side zooms or loops to the point?)

2. Does this frustrate either side? How?

3. How much of your reasoning style is necessitated by your job, and how much is due to personal preference?

4. How can you change your style to help prevent these frustrations?

Communication Style

Rational or Emotional

0	1	2	3	4	5	6	7	8	9	10

Rational ◄──────────────────────────────────► Emotional

• It's best to hide your emotions. • Feelings should play no part in persuasion or negotiation.	• It's best to show your emotions. • Passion and feeling show the importance of your argument and are valued.

The American style is somewhere toward the left end of this scale. Some Southeast Asians also prefer to keep their emotions in check when discussing something or presenting an idea.

Russians are notoriously far to the right of this scale, pounding fists (or shoes!) on tables to make their points, as are Arabs and most Mediterraneans, for example, Italians and Greeks.

Years ago I saw a news clip of some international relief workers delivering sacks of grain to Ethiopians during a famine in that country. I could tell that the Ethiopians were delighted to receive the help by the way they were jumping up and down with tears of joy. I *know* that if there were a food shortage in, say, Chicago and the locals received a shipment of grain, we would *never* see them behaving this way.

Certainly not in front of television cameras! There might be a somber interview clip of a Chicagoan saying something such as "It's very nice to receive this support—we can really use it here in Chicago."

How much emotion should you display when trying to convince someone or when expressing yourself? My experience with other cultures indicates that it's better to make the mistake of showing too little than to err by showing too much. Pay close attention to the level of emotion expressed by your international colleagues and, without tossing good judgment to the wind, try to match it when you deal with them. If you've read that Filipinos are quiet and nonconfrontational until they feel really provoked or cornered (at which time they explode with emotion), I don't recommend you try to incorporate a few emotional explosions into your coaching style. Be cautious about increasing your emotional intensity as you try different strategies, because you can never take back your words. In any event, a polite and professional manner is safest, but don't belittle emotional arguments.

Application

1. How do you react to major events (pick any example)—with emotion or in a rational and controlled manner?

2. Is your persuasive style more toward the emotional or the rational? How about your international counterparts' style?

3. Do you respect the styles of communication and persuasion that are different from yours?

4. Are there ways you might benefit either by toning down your emotional style or by carefully adding a bit more feeling to your argument?

Physical Space

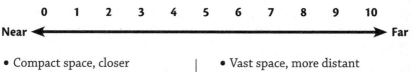

| 0 | 1 | 2 | 3 | 4 | 5 | 6 | 7 | 8 | 9 | 10 |

Near ←————————————————————————→ Far

- Compact space, closer interaction, nearer distances
- Vast space, more distant interaction, greater distances

Near and far are not really polar opposites, but this category makes a simple point: The amount of physical space people occupy, and the physical distance they maintain between themselves when interacting, vary across cultures.

Two things are likely to happen to Americans. First, we are likely to feel our space is being invaded by South Americans or Middle Easterners, who like to stand much closer than we are used to or feel comfortable with. Arabs like to get so close that they can smell your breath (and vice versa). As I mentioned earlier, try not to back up or betray your discomfort.

Second, Americans are likely to stand out overseas because of the large amount of space we use and because of the volume of our voices. Many Americans don't realize that we allow ourselves to take up lots of space with our bodies. American men, particularly, like to sprawl. They may cross their legs by putting an ankle on the opposite knee or stretch their legs out straight and cross their ankles (versus European and South American men, who cross their legs by putting one knee on top of the other). When they walk, many Americans swing their arms and generally occupy a lot of space, again, particularly men. Americans also tend to violate space rules by putting their feet up on train benches, chairs, or their own desks. I also want to add volume in this section, because it's related to space. With more vast spaces between them, American speakers might tend to talk loudly—and they often do.

The general rule, once again, is that you should observe and adapt to the ways in which people from other cultures use space, their voices, and their bodies.

Application

1. Can you identify any ways in which space plays a role in your interactions? Have you ever felt your space invaded? Have you ever been aware of invading someone else's space?

2. Be aware of the volume of your voice when talking to your international associates. Is it lower or higher than theirs?

Comfort with Silence

0	1	2	3	4	5	6	7	8	9	10

Embrace Silence   **Avoid Silence**

- Silence is respected and appreciated, with no discomfort attached.

- Silence causes people to feel edgy, uncomfortable.

Most Americans are comfortable with only about four seconds of silence during a meeting or conversation. Try this at a meeting or if you're presenting something in front of a group: finish a sentence and then remain silent for ten seconds. Many people aren't able to do it! After about six seconds (at the maximum) people will wonder what you are doing and will begin to fidget. If you continue to remain silent, someone will break the silence by speaking.

Once when I was presenting a program to a group of Japanese businesspeople, I paused to ask if they had any questions. Because I knew how silence can be used differently across cultures, I remained quiet while they considered the question. After about forty seconds (yes, *forty* seconds), one participant turned to his neighbor and began speaking in Japanese. He spoke for about thirty seconds; then the best English speaker at the table announced, "He has a question about some material three slides back."

If I had not taken the time to wait those forty seconds, which seemed an eternity to me, I would never have heard his question.

A Canadian emergency room doctor told me he was exasperated by the use of silence by Canadian Aboriginals (that's the Canadian term used instead of *Indian*). Emergency rooms are busy places and this doctor would whisk into each patient's room, glance at the chart, and ask, "Well, what do we have here?" The Canadian Aboriginals would react to his question with a long pause. They like to think before they speak, and silence doesn't bother them. But this silence was exasperating for this busy doctor, who frequently had a long line of other patients who needed urgent care.

> **Fifteen seconds can seem like fifteen minutes in a hospital emergency room!**

Another point worth mentioning here is that silence (or near silence) doesn't always mean no communication is taking place. For example, the Japanese are known for adding a "hmmm" or an "ah" or a "yes." You can gain a lot of information by noticing a person's tone of voice, eyes, face, body language, and posture even if all he is saying is "hmmm."

Application

1. Have you ever been frustrated by intentional silence? How could this be resolved?

2. If you feel uncomfortable with silence, how might this be difficult for those who prefer it? How might you modify your style to meet theirs?

Flow of Conversation

0	1	2	3	4	5	6	7	8	9	10

← ─── →

Interrupting (Fast)   Taking Turns (Medium)   Halting (Slow)

Every country follows different rules for who talks when and how they talk. If you've been dealing internationally, you will have already noticed that some conversations click and others don't. If we don't feel comfortable when talking to the other person, we will probably not be able to build much of a viable business relationship. On the following pages are three communication styles that will help to explain the various ways conversations flow in different countries as well as what makes them click or not.

Taking Turns. In the United States, English-speaking Canada, Australia, New Zealand, and Britain, conversational partners or people in a small group or a meeting take turns speaking.

It can be a real turnoff for English speakers from these countries if someone interrupts them before they are done speaking. It can also be awkward if someone expects the English speaker to interrupt and say something but the English speaker holds back, waiting patiently for the other person to finish.

Interrupting. This is the style of South American, Mediterranean European (such as in Spain, southern France, or Italy), Northern

African, and Middle Eastern people. A video conferencing company in Brazil had some initial "technical difficulties" because often several people in the meetings would talk at the same time. The problem arose because the camera was designed to rotate and focus on whomever was talking (it would hone in on the source of the sound). With several people talking at once, the camera would rotate erratically from person to person as it tried to locate the speaker. In order for the camera technology to work as designed,

It can be a real turnoff for English speakers from these countries if someone interrupts them before they are done speaking.

the Brazilians needed to modify their behavior such that only one person talked at a time while the others waited their turns.

On the other side of the coin, I learned early while living in France that if I waited for the other person to finish speaking, I'd never get a word in edgewise! I informally interviewed French people about this and concluded the following about our mismatch in conversation styles: I had at first thought that by interrupting me, the French didn't care about or agree with what I had to say. But my failure to "break in" to the conversation had led them to think that I had nothing to contribute or that I didn't care. Neither of these was true, of course. We were simply experiencing a mismatch of styles.

Once I understood this, I learned to be bolder with interruptions. There are little tricks the French (and many others) use to wedge their way into a conversation. One is to simply start speaking before the other person has finished. Or they open their mouth as though they're about to begin speaking, maybe lean forward, inhale, raise their eyebrows, or begin to gesture with their hands as if to make a point. If you don't feel comfortable simply interrupting, use these nonverbal clues to show that you have something to say; the person or people you're speaking with will be very ready to hear you the moment you begin to

talk. Pay attention to these and other similar body language clues people give to show they want to speak.

Halting. Because they are comfortable with silence, Asians and Native Americans can converse in what is perceived as a halting manner. This is where Person A talks, both pause to reflect, then Person B makes a comment, or Person A adds more to the original statement. Then Person A reflects for a few seconds before responding, and so on. These pauses for reflection can be off-putting for those who crack under the pressure of four seconds of silence and *need to say something*!

I say this *can* be the Asian (or Native American) style because it is not always the case. I have known Japanese, Chinese, and Koreans to be rapid-fire conversationalists at meals or in social settings, especially after a couple of drinks. It seems that everyone is talking at once, as you might expect of Latin Americans.

The rules for talking described in this section are not unrelated to those in the previous section where I described how some people go straight to the point and others circle or wander toward the point. As you might guess, people who take turns speaking are the ones who are likely to be concise and want to follow a straight line of thinking, whereas those who interrupt each other or proceed haltingly might be more tolerant of wandering toward or circling around the point.

Application

1. Which of the three communication styles (taking turns, interrupting, or halting) is closest to your own?

2. Has this created conflicts? How? How can these conflicts be resolved? Who should change?

3. Pay attention to how your international associates tend to interrupt or not interrupt one another. Are there ways you could participate more in conversations by learning how to appropriately interject yourself into a conversation? Are there ways in which you push too much in conversations and don't allow others to participate?

Part 5

Knowing Your Cultural Style

"Culture schmulture! People are basically the same around the world and I don't need to know any 'culture stuff,' as an American. They can learn my culture, right?"

Wrong! And workplaces with international mixes know it better than anyone. In the United States we have significant populations from everywhere in the world: Africa, Asia, South America, Europe, and so on. Even where I am from—Minnesota, which is in the center of our huge continent—we have a cultural mix, and it will continue to grow. In every corner of the U.S. the locals like to point out that there are even differences among the neighboring towns. There are even greater differences between Wisconsin and Texas, New York and California, or Florida and Oregon. If you think along these lines, you can easily recognize that the British or European way of doing things will be quite different from the American way, and this is even more the case when the American way is compared with the Asian or Middle Eastern way.

Differing Cultural Styles Lead to Clashes

International cultural differences matter because they affect everything people do. Among other things, cultural programming affects

- how dedicated people will be to work (remember before how I noted that the French government mandated a thirty-five-hour maximum workweek?),

- how quickly people will respond to faxes or e-mails (in places such as fast-paced Singapore and the United States, people expect—and demand—immediate responses),

- how comfortable people will be making changes (we thrive on change in the United States; many Japanese don't),

- how people make decisions (by giving commands, building consensus, or deciding by vote),

- how formal people are (we're usually on a first-name basis in the United States; Germans and others are frequently not), and

- how people communicate (getting straight to business is the U.S. style; many others work on patiently building relationships first).

These are just six of many examples reflecting business style. But combine these six examples into one scenario and they add up: (1) You zoom an e-mail to a European distributor who is either on vacation or not working overtime to meet your demands as you had hoped because (2) you need a quick response regarding what you think is (3) a simple change in the order process. Unfortunately, your European distributor (4) cannot decide this alone because he needs to confer with his boss on most decisions, and besides, (5) he felt treated like a child when you wrote "Hi Frank" instead of "Dear Mr. Schubert," and (6) because your e-mail itself had no introduction, no courtesies, and no closing, it seemed to him like an offensively blatant *demand*.

Have you ever wanted to strangle a co-worker who whistles? These "office whistlers" are usually happy and blissfully unaware that they could even be bothering anyone with their whistling. The next time you find yourself thinking "Bah! Culture schmulture!" consider that you may have some international co-workers (or customers, clients, partners) who may want to strangle you because of your natural (and happy but blissfully unaware) cultural style!

You Have a Culture

I've just described how the cultural style that works for you at home can naturally lead to clashes when dealing with people from other cultures. When I present thoughts like this to people in my workshops, usually people nod their heads and seem to relate. Yet at the same time as they seem to be agreeing with what I've said, many of them think that it somehow doesn't apply to them. No matter where you're from, and even if you think you're just a local like everyone else, I assure you that you do indeed have a culture and your style does matter.

Me? I don't have a culture; I'm just like all the locals here...

You Also Have a Communication Style

Because you have a body, body language is a part of your communication style. Because you have a voice, you use tone and inflection. And because you have a personality, it must come across in the way you speak, and because you have a cultural style, I can guarantee you that it, plus your beliefs, your worldview, and your individual quirks come across when you communicate. This is a good thing, because without these individual traits, we would all sound like some sort of standardized robot.

But we're not robots, and our communication is fluid and unpredictable. Some linguists have built flowcharts of topics that people might be likely to follow in a conversation, but I am proposing something a little different: what we choose to say and how we choose to say it are tricky to predict or explain. For example, think back to the last conversation you had. Do you know why you said what you did? Can you explain or justify each thing you said? Unless you were using a teleprompter or being fed responses from an earpiece, you were inventing what to say as you went along, sometimes directing the flow of subjects

Does continually nodding your head mean you agree?

yourself, sometimes following your partner's lead. How could you possibly give someone else instructions for what to say in a similar conversation? We each have to make it up as we go.

What we say and how we say it depend on who we are, both individually and culturally. As individuals, we might be extroverted or introverted, knowledgeable or ignorant, cheerful or irritable, defensive or empathetic, and so on. These factors make communication very unpredictable. As you've learned, national cultural differences affect communication, too. Obviously, just knowing that someone is from a particular country doesn't mean we can predict his or her communication style. Every situation is different, and an irritable Italian will respond to you differently from one who's in a positive mood. Still, it can be helpful to understand a bit about communication styles. Below are some themes that can vary according to culture.

- *Direct/indirect:* method of giving feedback, conflict style, levels of openness in discussion, face, and so forth, as described in Parts 1 and 4

- *Physical distance:* whether we stand close or far, how much space we take up with gestures and with our bodies

- *Eye contact:* how direct eye contact is interpreted—as a challenge, as honesty, as deference

- *Verbal:* intonation, volume, pace, accents or dialects, tone

- *Nonverbal communication:* gestures, posture, use of silence, nodding

- *Conversation flow:* interrupting, taking turns, halting

- *Level of formality:* use of title plus last name versus first name, power issues such as not interrupting the boss

Some of these have been mentioned in previous sections, but consider them together within the context of your own communication style. Recall the bullet points at the beginning of this section showing how what we could call an "American style" (expecting a quick response to an e-mail, being informal) can lead to clashes with those whose styles are different. How does your style fit in the list above?

Awareness of others needs to start with self-awareness. Over several years of visiting, living, and working in France, I learned something important about French conversational style that's very different from my own American style: Americans are continually nodding their heads, with eyebrows raised in a friendly way, perhaps smiling as if to constantly send the message, "Yes! Yes! I'm listening! I agree! I'm friendly! I'm not going to hurt you!" This is how Americans show that they care about the conversation (or at least pretend they do).

The Frenchwoman vigorously protested, interrupting me with "Je ne suis pas d'accord!" ("I totally disagree!")

Over time I became aware that the French operate quite differently. In French conversation it's important to disagree. Disagreeing can show that you are actively listening and that you are thinking carefully about what you are hearing. There isn't necessarily any animosity involved.

What is a natural conversation style in France might be seen as a rude conversation stopper in the United States. But when the French tell you they disagree and tell you why, they will often indeed point out something valuable that you had not considered.

In conducting a cross-cultural program for a couple transferring to France, I was explaining this French tendency to disagree. As part of the program, a Frenchwoman was at the table with us adding many helpful comments. I was explaining to the Americans that the French often disagree openly in conversation. The Frenchwoman vigorously protested, interrupting me with "I totally disagree!" After a moment of silence, all of us around the table (including the Frenchwoman) burst into laughter! The Frenchwoman had unwittingly proven me right by her behavior. She disagreed that the French disagree!

The section "Flow of Conversation" in Part 4 introduced different ways of interrupting, taking turns, or using a halting pace. I encourage you to evaluate these dimensions as well as the other topics in the section "People and Communication Issues" in Part 4 and to apply them to both your own communication style and to that of the specific country and situations you are dealing with. There are entire books on communication style if you wish to explore this issue further. (See Recommended Readings.)

Yes, Cultural Intelligence Is a Soft Skill

In spite of the fact that many people don't realize that they have cultural styles and communication styles, people persist in thinking that culture is no big deal. Some people reason, "That culture stuff is just a soft skill" or they think, "Just follow your intuition and you'll do okay overseas."

As I said in the Introduction, that's a little bit like saying, "The Beatles songs were really simple—just three chords and a little melody. I could probably sit down and write a half-dozen platinum hits in an afternoon."

The "numbers" professions, such as accounting, or the "hard sciences," such as engineering, are certainly crucial to business. These kinds of "hard skills" are necessary for business success. But equally important are the "soft skills" of human interaction that lead to excellent customer service and the ability to build trust. Cultural intelligence falls into this soft-skill category. Without these soft skills, deals are not signed, lasting partnerships are not formed, customers do not return, and so on. The face-to-face cultural skills that can make or break a business deal should definitely be considered important even if they are not the number-crunching or exacting type of hard skill.

Don't Rely on Local Amateurs

An important lesson in the story of the Frenchwoman disagreeing that the French will disagree is that people from any given place don't usually know a great deal about their own communication and cultural styles or how these impact on any variety of issues from greeting behaviors to general business approaches to leading multinational teams to opinions about the importance of work versus leisure time. Talking to people from another culture (like the Frenchwoman) can be interesting, even enlightening, but don't expect them to be experts on their culture just because they were born or raised there, as the following examples from cross-cultural workshops illustrate:

- A Russian woman pounded her fist on the table and loudly insisted, "Russians are not loud and boisterous!"

- One Filipino argued that the family is not at all important in the Philippines. "More people can get divorced now, and things are changing in the Philippines," he reasoned. His argument was perhaps weakened slightly by the fact that he lived under the same roof with three generations of family.

- A Japanese participant said, "No no, Japan is not at all a 'work society'...in fact we have a lot of fun drinking and going out with our co-workers after work—sometimes until very late at night." Many might say that only in a work-oriented society would you be with your co-workers until midnight!

Of course, locals from anywhere love to *think* they are cultural experts, and after all, they *do* know something about where they are from, don't they? Of course they do, but few people can step back and play the role of a reliable and independent viewer of their own culture.

So if you shouldn't turn to locals for expertise on their own culture, whom should you turn to? Competent cross-cultural trainers can be good resources, but unfortunately there is no organization that certifies cross-cultural trainers, and it's up to you to choose a competent professional. "And just how am I supposed to do that?" you ask. I recommend that you look for four basic qualifications in a cross-cultural trainer or consultant (in no order of importance):

Overseas Experience. Definitely don't hire someone who has never been outside his or her own country except to do intercultural training

sessions or workshops at confer-
ences. Make sure your resource
person has lived extensively
overseas and, if possible, has
been to the country or at least
the region you are focusing on.
No cross-cultural trainer will
be old enough to have spent a
decade in the twenty separate

> **I can't help but chuckle at the "sideline experts" who, while watching others play chess, will say, "Oh. I wouldn't have made *that* move!"**

countries he or she might conduct programs about, but should have at
least some "below-the-waterline" international/intercultural experience with the general region you are dealing with. A good cross-cultural
coach who has been to your target region can use local resource people
to offer a well-rounded program.

Academic Qualifications. Does the person know the foundational
theories as well as the current trends in the cross-cultural field? It's
important to have a resource person who can make practical sense of
relevant theories, knowledge, and information.

Business Savvy. Three master's degrees and a Ph.D. might seem adequate, but theory has to have practical application, and I recommend
that you select cross-cultural resource people who have basic business
or professional experience and accompanying insights in areas such
as negotiating, international teams, management, marketing, sales,
advertising, the various aspects of the due diligence process, customer
service, or whatever other areas may be relevant to your international
efforts.

Education/Coaching Skills. I've spent a bit of time in academia both
as a student and in my career as a professor. One of my pet peeves has
been the too-common myth that anyone with an overhead projector
and a mouth is qualified to "teach." The process of education or coaching takes finesse, expertise, and wisdom. It also takes time; too often
clients want a trainer who can condense a cross-cultural initiative into
a single four- or eight-hour block of information. A successful cross-
cultural consultant or educator will know how to manage this delicate
learning process over time, and you as the client should insist on it.

Whether or not you have access to cross-cultural training, I suggest that you tap other sources, such as the multitude of good books
and articles on other countries. The Appendix and the Recommended

Readings section at the end of the book list some examples of published culture-general books and Internet sources you might explore. There are also numerous Websites at your fingertips for country-specific information.

No matter whom you choose as an expert on your target culture or which sources you use, be sure you have a strategic plan for understanding how your international clients, distributors, or partners think, work, live, behave, believe, make decisions, manage, and so on. Of these, the amateur has no real knowledge. I also recommend that you learn about specific socioeconomic, historical, and geopolitical issues as well as essential foreign phrases. I indicate in Part 6 how to acquire practical knowledge of these matters.

The more knowledgeable you are, the more the competitive advantage you'll have when building international business relationships. Do you disagree? (How French of you!)

Below, I will present some ways of knowing your own strengths and weaknesses.

Traits for Success

Part of knowing our own cultural style is knowing our strengths and weaknesses related to international interactions. Common sense tells us that there are certain skills and personality traits that will lead to successful interaction overseas. When you are going through the occasional "blues" of culture shock on an assignment abroad or facing a challenging international interaction, it will obviously help if you are the kind of person who can talk to people easily. Being outgoing (or deciding to act in an outgoing manner even if you don't feel like it) may be a plus in such situations.

Open-mindedness is another trait that most people would obviously agree is useful for international professionals. No one would deliberately choose their most stubbornly opinionated employee to represent the company in an intercultural environment.

We might try to develop a test to measure traits or skills such as extroversion or open-mindedness. The difficulty with developing such a test is that you can easily fake your way through it. Let's try it: How would you respond to a question like this if you wanted a good score?

"I like to try new things."   *Strongly agree / Strongly disagree*

Obviously, you'd answer "Strongly agree" for a higher score. Because they would be so easy to "psych out," my concern is that tests like this would not be valid. For example, you couldn't legitimately use such a test for choosing which person should go or not go on an international assignment. Any test depending on honesty in this way would have obvious limitations. When assessing yourself (or someone else) on topics like this, relevance and validity come when you honestly apply the questions to your own specific situations and when you expose your own perceived strengths and weaknesses to the feedback of your colleagues. With such feedback, as well as with a desire to coax your weaknesses into strengths, you can improve. That said, let's at least informally examine eleven traits or competencies for dealing with people from other countries, whether you are in their country or they are in yours.

Cultural Self-Awareness. The first critical step is cultural self-awareness. On one hand, you can't learn about other people's cultures until you develop awareness of

> **Use other cultures as a mirror to see your own.**

your own. On the other hand, we gain the best cultural self-awareness after actually traveling to other countries and engaging in firsthand experiences with different peoples and their values and attitudes, their worldviews, their way of life, and so forth. Self-awareness and awareness of others are built in an ever-increasing cycle, each enhancing the other. The most concise and straightforward advice I can give for learning about your own cultural makeup is to travel internationally.

Cultural Awareness of Others. This relates to the knowledge of the various components of differences among people from different cultures and countries. Again, knowing about something doesn't mean you'll be able to do it, but it's an important second step in deciding how you might change your behavior to become more effective. (Topics such as the categories discussed in Part 3 can serve as a map for increasing your awareness.) From here on, cultural awareness of and sensitivity to other cultures reinforces cultural self-awareness and vice versa.

Cultural Sensitivity. This suggests an attitude of respect and acceptance coupled with the skills to put your acceptance into practice in specific ways. It's important to remember that sensitivity is more than an attitude; it must be demonstrated through behavior. Recall the last time you considered someone to be insensitive; I imagine you were reacting to specific behavior you perceived as negative. Conversely, sensitivity to other cultures must be demonstrated through positive behavior showing genuine acceptance of or interest in another's culture. I use the word *sensitivity* here rather than *tolerance* because tolerance may imply "putting up with" someone, whereas sensitivity more likely involves not judging that culture.

Cross-cultural Communication Skills. These are a set of appropriate verbal and nonverbal skills translating into behaviors—both spoken and written—face to face, over the phone, or in written correspondence. This could mean knowing what to write in an e-mail and when and how to write it, or it could mean the ability to successfully manage an international negotiation.

Tolerance for Ambiguity. The ability to deal with ambiguity could be considered beneficial in any field, but rest assured that you will have more opportunities to be surprised by the totally unfamiliar and the undecipherable in international mixes. Ambiguities are inevitable when people communicate in other languages and cultural styles. It's dangerous to make assumptions when relating with people from one's own culture, but this is even more problematic when interacting with people from other cultures.

What leads to the most confusing situations is when we fail to even recognize that misunderstandings have occurred. We then continue under the illusion that both we and our international counterparts understand one another when actually one or both sides may not. Such unrecognized misunderstandings, which persist precisely because they are not recognized, eventually result in one or both sides making surprising or even totally incongruous moves. When this happens, *befuddlement* might be a better choice of words than *ambiguity*, and it's these unrecognized misunderstandings that successful international professionals have learned how to recover from.

Flexibility. Another general skill that is required more often in international mixes is flexibility. This can mean any variety of things: adjusting to different foods, typing on a different keyboard, or using a different phone system. It can also mean changing the way you interview patients or greet customers. It can mean adjusting learning to move business more slowly or more quickly, with less or more information and preparation.

I only drive Buicks, never eat spicy food, and prefer a firm pillow. Those Latinos sure don't know how to live!

Open-mindedness. As mentioned several pages ago, open-mindedness is a very useful trait. International mixes offer us many occasions to be confronted by new ways of thinking and living that we don't agree with and that we personally would not choose. As we go through life, we make choices and know what works for us and what doesn't. Based on our experience, we develop strong preferences about what we want—or don't want. How shocking it can be to see that others have made different choices! I don't like being challenged to open my mind. Who does? It's a process that ranges from being slightly uncomfortable to being excruciating. But the more open-minded we are, the more quickly we can move from demanding "Why do these people do things this way?" to realizing that others' lifestyles and behaviors make perfect sense for them in their cultural context.

Humility. My positive experiences with clients suggest that a sense of humility often develops in many people engaged in international mixes, but it does not develop immediately or without a few painful knocks. And, unfortunately, it sometimes does not develop at all; instead, a sour attitude or sense of chauvinism (in the sense of unreasonably exaggerated patriotism) comes about instead. One barrier to humility is that the manager, director, executive, or other professional who is domestically successful is often shocked to find that he or she does not rule the roost and command respect in international surroundings.

Empathy. The capacity for empathy could be considered the intersection among several of the categories I've mentioned: awareness of others, cultural sensitivity, and humility. The ability to empathize, that is, put yourself in your international counterpart's shoes (and walk a mile in them), reinforces these traits and may change your perception about a person's behavior or a situation. As with these other traits, a person's level of empathy cannot really be tested objectively.

Outgoing Personality. It may sound simplistic but an outgoing personality, as mentioned earlier, contributes to international success. When two people share a common language and common cultural perspectives, it can be easy to make a connection. When these are lacking, interactions can be awkward, and it's natural to avoid situations where we feel awkward.

Are you socially fearless?

So the simple ability to initiate or join a conversation can indeed be an important skill, leading to successful international interactions. While personality traits such as extroversion or introversion may be innate and to some extent unchangeable, it's also possible to deliberately work to change our behaviors (become more extroverted). Those who can take the plunge and talk easily to people from other cultures have a clear edge over those who hold back to avoid feeling uncomfortable.

Self-Reliance. An especially useful character trait in overseas settings is self-reliance, because the support of colleagues and the resources of the home office are not easily accessible. Unless one has a twenty-four-hour butler and tour guide, surviving (and thriving) in unfamiliar settings is an act which inherently requires self-reliance. Overseas, many of the supportive and familiar factors from home may be lacking: social settings, food, ways of relaxing after work, and ways of doing things, from getting around town (or out of town) to buying basic supplies. In the new environment, the necessity to act independently is far greater.

On the next page I propose a simple table for ranking yourself in the above traits. Yes, you might say, I can psych this test out, too. Of course you can, but what good will that do you? Labeling those characteristics as strengths or not strengths is meant to encourage you to be honest with yourself and to see what traits you need to develop more. Besides, you don't need to share this assessment with anyone. Use it to help build your strengths.

Quick Intercultural Self-Assessment

	Not a Strength	Somewhat of a Strength	Significant Strength
Cultural self-awareness			
Cultural awareness (of others)			
Cultural sensitivity			
Cross-cultural communication skills			
Tolerance for ambiguity			
Flexibility			
Open-mindedness			
Humility			
Empathy			
An outgoing personality			
Self-reliance			

If you work on a team, it is useful to complete this self-assessment as a group, but keep in mind that this is a high-risk activity requiring trust among the team members. It's completely acceptable for two people to interpret the same category in different ways. In fact, discussing team members' varying perceptions of the same categories can bring new insights. It can also be useful to know where your team members' strengths lie. Again, this will only work for a team that has developed a high degree of trust.

If it's relevant to your situation, I recommend using this quick tool to collect "360-degree feedback"; that is, if you're serious about getting a more honest profile, ask people working above you, below you, and at your level to rank *you* in these categories—but be prepared for possibly unpleasant surprises. This kind of feedback is only successful when participants don't fear reprisals.

Of course the process of seeking feedback from others would also need to be managed by a competent facilitator who can also make specific recommendations. But it is through the process of sharing feedback that these assessments take on validity. Knowing that your co-workers will hold you accountable for your answers may encourage you to be more honest about your strengths and weaknesses! If you like, you can connect the Xs you've marked in each column to give a quick visual overview to compare with others' self-rankings. You could also use different colors to rank one another on each other's charts.

What Is Your Cultural Style?

Next I list the five cultural scales from Part 1 and the nineteen dimensions from Part 4. I suggest you rank yourself on all five culture scales from Part 1 and then on those from Part 4 that are the most relevant to your work situation (not all will apply to everyone).

Here's how I suggest you proceed. First put a dot where you would rank on the scales.* (Actually draw it on the page!) You can also put dots representing your co-workers,

> **The first step for increasing cultural intelligence is to know your own style.**

international counterparts, customers, and so forth. It doesn't matter which culture they come from. You might use a dot for yourself, a D for the Dutch office, an L for the Latino sales department, an H for Hiroko the Japanese distributor, and so forth. Make your own key any way you wish. Based on your situation and what you might find useful, you could rank groups (e.g., one dot for the entire Malaysian sales office) or individuals (e.g., a dot for Herb, the German manager). If you're doing this with others, it's helpful to make rankings privately first, compare them afterward, and then discuss implications.

---

* If you want a more reliable way of ranking yourself than just putting dots on the chart, and if you want specific suggestions based on the difference between your ranking and the profiles of various target countries, see the Appendix for information on the *Peterson Cultural Style Indicator,*™ which offers you a definitive profile of your cultural style.

No matter which ranking approach you use, be aware that the actual number for a person or group is not the most important thing. There's no point dickering over whether the Singaporeans are 8.4 or 9.6 on a given scale. What matters most is to what degree and in which direction they are different from you. That is, if your Singaporean colleague is toward the right of center on a given scale and you are toward the left, this will indicate some possible differences in the way you might prefer to manage, work, make decisions, handle conflicts, and so forth. Parts 1 and 4 discussed some of these differences. After you complete the rankings, you may want to revisit those parts.

Here is the basic framework from Part 1 describing cultural style. Rank yourself and anyone else you wish:

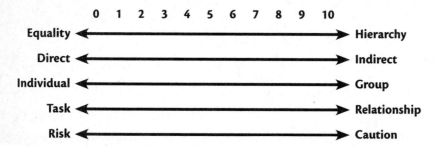

	0	1	2	3	4	5	6	7	8	9	10	
Equality	←										→	Hierarchy
Direct	←										→	Indirect
Individual	←										→	Group
Task	←										→	Relationship
Risk	←										→	Caution

Below are the categories from Part 4. Proceed with the rankings.

Role of Managers

0	1	2	3	4	5	6	7	8	9	10

"The Boss" ←→ "Team Player"

Decision-Making Style

0	1	2	3	4	5	6	7	8	9	10

Consensus ← Collaborative → Command

Conflict Style

0	1	2	3	4	5	6	7	8	9	10

Direct ←→ Indirect

Work Style

| 0 | 1 | 2 | 3 | 4 | 5 | 6 | 7 | 8 | 9 | 10 |

Multitask   Monotask

Employee Motivation and Rewards

| 0 | 1 | 2 | 3 | 4 | 5 | 6 | 7 | 8 | 9 | 10 |

Personal   Impersonal

Work Priorities

| 0 | 1 | 2 | 3 | 4 | 5 | 6 | 7 | 8 | 9 | 10 |

Live to Work   Work to Live

Views on Change

| 0 | 1 | 2 | 3 | 4 | 5 | 6 | 7 | 8 | 9 | 10 |

Positive   Negative

Level of Control over Life and Business

| 0 | 1 | 2 | 3 | 4 | 5 | 6 | 7 | 8 | 9 | 10 |

In Control   Not in Control

Quality

| 0 | 1 | 2 | 3 | 4 | 5 | 6 | 7 | 8 | 9 | 10 |

Aesthetic   Functional

Planning Style

| 0 | 1 | 2 | 3 | 4 | 5 | 6 | 7 | 8 | 9 | 10 |

Ready, Aim, Fire   Ready, Fire, Aim

Freedom versus Identity

0   1   2   3   4   5   6   7   8   9   10

Freedom   Identity

Pace of Life

0   1   2   3   4   5   6   7   8   9   10

Time as Scarce   Time as Plentiful

Courtesy, Protocol, Formality

0   1   2   3   4   5   6   7   8   9   10

Informal   Formal

Reasoning Styles

Start with the   Arrive at the   Finish with the
conclusion   conclusion all   conclusion
                        at once

Cognitive Style and Communication

0   1   2   3   4   5   6   7   8   9   10

Linear   Circular

Rational or Emotional Communication

0   1   2   3   4   5   6   7   8   9   10

Rational   Emotional

Physical Space

0   1   2   3   4   5   6   7   8   9   10

Near   Far

Comfort with Silence

| 0 | 1 | 2 | 3 | 4 | 5 | 6 | 7 | 8 | 9 | 10 |

Embrace Silence   **Avoid Silence**

Flow of Conversation

| 0 | 1 | 2 | 3 | 4 | 5 | 6 | 7 | 8 | 9 | 10 |

Interrupting   **Taking Turns**   **Halting**
(Fast)   **(Medium)**   **(Slow)**

Learning about Others' Cultural Styles

You now know that your professional relationships with people from other cultures will be improved if you know more about them. So how can you find out who someone is culturally? At the organizational level, your company or organization could decide to take the direct and strategic approach of having employees complete a culture profile and then ask them to compare their results with colleagues. Some companies take exactly this approach by having employees complete the Myers-Briggs Type Indicator, attend training sessions on it, and then even print employee profiles (e.g., "ENFP" or "ISTJ") on their company ID badges. The same can be done with cultural style (i.e., your badge might show you to be an "EDITR" for "Equality, Direct, Individual, Task, Risk"). A major initiative like this is, of course, not something all organizations would choose to invest the time and money that would be required.

> **Knowing your own style helps you know others'.**

A much simpler approach is learning about others at the level of individual personal interactions, and that's what I'll discuss here. When faced with the unfamiliar, our normal first reaction is discomfort and a strong desire to back away. When we are facing someone from another culture we don't know much about, we get nervous because we don't know what to say, and we can only run on about the weather or something equally nonthreatening for a limited time as we wonder how to end the conversation politely before we turn tail and run.

I remember one of my first conversations with a Bahamian who lived across the hall from me in college. He asked me about "playin' a box." A *box* was his slang word for a guitar, and he wanted to talk to me about the guitar I played—just to make conversation. I had no idea what box he was talking about at first, but I quickly put it together when he gestured playing a guitar. I remember it as an awkward conversation, but I also remember that from that conversation I wasn't going to perish from fright or be bored to tears by sticking around and talking to him about the "box." I also realized I could learn some interesting things about him and the Bahamas by overcoming that first awkwardness. Instead of avoiding this guy the next time I saw him, I purposely stopped and talked to him to see what I could learn about him and the culture he was from.

It's not always possible to tell where someone is from by his or her appearance. I have Asian American friends who are racially Asian but culturally and linguistically American. I am careful to not make the mistake of assuming that an "Asian-looking" person is Asian.

> **Impress people with your inquisitive mind, not your vast knowledge.**

An accent can, but does not always, indicate that someone is from another country. Many of our fellow citizens have foreign accents. When I detect a foreign accent when I meet someone, I view it as a possible opportunity to learn more through a little personal research! But because I figure people with accents must hear the question "Where ya from?" so often, I try to refrain from blurting it out when I first meet someone. Instead, I try to work an opportunity to inquire into our conversation.

I encourage you to do the same. Once you know your conversation partner's country of origin, if you are interested, find out what you can. If you know a woman is from Gambia, ask her what life is like in Gambia. If you don't know where Gambia is, by all means ask her! Don't try to play it smart. I think that if you want to impress people, you'll do better with your inquisitive mind than with a list of facts you've memorized.

If you run into a Gambian man who's willing to talk about his own culture, ask him what language he speaks. "You speak seven of them?" "How is that possible?" "What are they?" "In what context do you use each one?" "What was your biggest shock when you first arrived?" "What do you miss most about home?" The point is that most people *love* to talk about themselves and usually feel flattered that you are interested in them—as long as you don't come on too strong. Note: I'm not suggesting that you ask about your new acquaintance's sex life, religious beliefs, or income. Use your good judgment and ask a few informal questions as you play the role of "diplomat" and "humble culture researcher." At the same time, pay close attention to your acquaintance's nonverbal behavior; if you sense you have put your foot in your mouth, change your line of questioning.

With some clients I use a series of questions as a team-building activity for people who don't know each other. Partners or small groups get together and answer the question "Who are you?" I ask them to respond without referring to what they do (for work). This is a challenge, as I mentioned briefly in Part 1 in the discussion of task versus relationship, and it can be especially tough for task-focused Americans. Sometimes when I'm asking a group of people to go around the table and introduce themselves, their answers will look like this:

Person 1:	I'm Jim. I work in accounting. I take care of all the payroll paperwork. Mostly I work with the lawnmower and small engine division, but I'm beginning to work more with the flowerpot division.
Person 2:	I'm Linda. I'm in sales. My job is mostly to send faxes all over the world to communicate with our distributors.
Brooks:	I'm Brooks. I come from a long line of poor Swedish and Norwegian farmers and laborers. I feel that in life it's important to always be learning something new no matter what age I am. For example, I might decide to take up piano when I'm seventy.

Of course I get some strange looks if I continue to talk like this. But when you think of it, isn't it even stranger that when I ask people to tell me who they *are*, they tell me what they *do*? That is my point.

So try the following activity with your team or in small groups or pairs. If you have a culturally mixed group, you are guaranteed to get interesting answers which, if followed up, will lead to interesting insights about who the person is "culturally" and where he or she falls in several cultural dimensions. I routinely use questions like those below for intercultural team building. The questions seem simple, but the answers offer real cultural insights! It's easy to see at first glance that questions such as numbers 7, 8, or 9 (below) ask most directly about a person's cultural style. But I believe it's impossible to answer any of these questions sufficiently without exposing some element of cultural style. Try discussing these in pairs or in combinations of co-workers as you see fit. I recommend allowing people at least thirty minutes to discuss these questions together. This can be an awkward process, so it is important that the questions be asked in a non-threatening way. I would point out here that questions you consider appropriate may shock others. And others may shock you with their questions. For example, asking about one's income or why one is not married is considered quite appropriate in some cultures but intrusive and rude in others. Finally, because people are more comfortable with someone they know, I recommend that you pair up with someone you don't know very well to discuss these items; you'll learn more.

1. What was the most interesting period of your life? Why?

2. What was the most difficult period of your life? Why?

3. Answer the question "Who are you?" without referring to your occupation.

4. What is an issue you feel strongly about?

5. What was an important event in your life?

6. What do you imagine your life will be like in five years?

7. Name five adjectives that describe most people you like. Why do you like these attributes?

8. How do you define friendship?

9. How do you define "living well"? How do you define "success"?

10. Do you work to live, or do you live to work? Describe what you mean.

11. Do you have a purpose in life? If so, what is it?

12. What have you done successfully in your life?

The preceding questions are useful for getting to know people you deal with directly, especially counterparts from other countries whom you see routinely and trust.

Insularity Is Never Self-Proclaimed!

A final comment I want to make in this section is that people rarely say, "Gee—I'm really closed-minded. I don't know how to talk to foreigners, and I'm suspicious of almost everyplace in the world outside my own hometown!"

The term *insularity* means "having a narrow, provincial attitude about anything unfamiliar or different"—and implies wearing blinders. When we deal with culture issues, it's common to encounter such attitudes. Even worse are those people with an ethnocentric bent. They feel America is the best and the only, so why learn about other countries? Often, the people who most need to increase their cross-cultural awareness and skills don't realize it, don't think they need these skills. This can be eminently frustrating for the people who do "get it."

How many dunces are self-coronated?

I must admit I've sometimes fantasized about taking certain closed-minded individuals and buying them a one-way ticket to, oh, Burundi in the middle of Africa. I would be kind enough to give them a liter of fresh drinking water for their arrival there, but they would have no money and no return ticket, so if they ever wanted to make it home, they would be absolutely *obliged* to interact with someone incredibly different from themselves. They would be forced to learn a bit of a foreign language, to use body language, to modify their communication style, to listen attentively, to keep an open mind, and in general to undergo a bit of cultural evolution…or never get home.

The people I have the most fun working with are, of course, the people who do get it about culture. And when people do have a lot to learn and they realize it, they certainly don't need to feel humiliated for being where they are! Obviously, it's okay if people haven't ever traveled outside their home country, if they are insular or internationally inexperienced, as long as they make an honest effort to broaden their experiences and their minds by becoming internationally involved in some way.

Part 6

Increasing Your Cultural Intelligence

Parts 1 through 4 have examined culture definitions and analogies, discussed why cultural awareness is inescapably important for international professionals today, defined cultural intelligence and discussed whether it can be increased. These earlier sections organized culture into five main scales and a number of minor ones relating to management issues, strategy issues, communication issues, and so forth. In Part 5 you ranked yourself on those various scales.

I assume at this point that you fully accept the premise that culture is important and recognize that cultural differences do exist and do matter greatly. I will also assume that you have a basic awareness of what culture is and understand the differences between the levels of culture, from surface issues to deeper, culture-based values and attitudes. No doubt as you have read this book you have made your own discoveries based on prior personal experiences encountering other cultures. And if you've made it this far, I can only take it for granted that you are motivated to study cultures.

Weaving Together the Strands

With all these strands identified, now in this final part of the book the question is: How do you weave them together to increase your cultural intelligence? What practical actions can you take to become a savvier international professional? What can you *do* about what you've read, heard about, thought about, and experienced firsthand? This emphasis on practical application, on how you can increase your cultural intelligence, is the focus of Part 6.

As I suggested with my juggling analogy in the Introduction, cultural intelligence involves three components. It involves aspects of knowledge (facts about places, economies, history, etc.), it involves awareness (knowing about yourself and others), and it involves skills (knowing how to *do* something).

Knowledge about Cultures (facts and cultural traits)
+ Awareness (of yourself and others)
+ Specific Skills (behaviors)
= Cultural Intelligence

Like the three legs of a tripod, all three components must be in place for cultural intelligence to grow.* When I defined culture and cultural intelligence and when I offered the iceberg analogy and presented five culture scales, I was suggesting specific bits of knowledge that are likely to help you increase your cultural intelligence. This knowledge is one leg of the cultural intelligence tripod. When I then suggested you rank yourself and your international counterparts on various culture scales, my intent was to help you increase awareness of areas of difference. This awareness of how and why conflicts or misunderstandings happen is a second necessary part of the cultural intelligence tripod. In this last part of the book I will suggest some very specific skills that can get you started on building the third leg of the tripod.

What kind of skills will Part 6 focus on? This book was designed for a very wide audience. An "international professional" could mean an import/export manager in the garment industry or it could mean a Canadian professor guest lecturing in the Netherlands for a semester. So although it might be very relevant to a very small number of specific

---

* I don't think it's very useful to ask which leg of the tripod must be addressed or learned first. All three legs of a tripod must simultaneously work together; just as cross-cultural knowledge, awareness, and skills are intertwined and contribute together to cultural intelligence. As you strengthen or increase one component of your cultural intelligence (such as your communication skills), others (such as new awarenesses) will follow. I like the tripod metaphor because it suggests three components required for inherent stability, but at the same time, unlike the legs of a stool, the three components of this cultural intelligence formula are intertwined and not separate.

readers, in this section I can't give you Italian lessons (though if you were an importer of Italian goods, some Italian language skills would come in handy and certainly contribute to cultural intelligence). Instead, I will offer some very specific suggestions that can be useful to any international professional and I will make some recommendations that will coach you toward increasing your skills in ways that you determine to be specifically relevant.

First, I will offer some suggestions on dealing with people who are different from you on the five basic culture scales presented in Part 1. Into those five I will blend a discussion of the nineteen other minor scales on which you ranked yourself and your colleagues in Part 5.

Then I will discuss how you can increase your cultural intelligence in three main areas: communication skills, practical working knowledge of a country, and a framework for considering international ethics issues. I focus on these three areas because they can form a solid base of skill and awareness for international professionals. Communication skills are invaluable, because nothing can make or break interpersonal interactions more easily than face-to-face contact. When discussing communication skills, I offer specific suggestions (specific behaviors) you can put into practice. My suggestions on building practical background knowledge of the target country are necessarily more abstract or conceptual. I hope to point you in the right direction for researching your target country and explain why I think it's the right direction, but it will then be up to you to find relevant, specific information. I close Part 6 with comments on ethics because whether you are engaged in international business at home or abroad, in diplomacy, or in serving diverse populations within your own culture, you will inevitably be required to make decisions involving people with culture-based value frameworks (i.e., the bottom-of-the-iceberg values, beliefs, attitudes, and philosophies discussed in Part 1) different from your own. In these situations it is very useful to have a basic framework to guide you in your decisions and interactions.

Dealing with Differences in the Five Scales

In Part 5 you had a chance to rank yourself and your international counterparts on two dozen scales (the five basic culture scales presented in Part 1 plus the nineteen other scales presented in Part 4). This should give you a better understanding of the directions in which cultural differences are likely to lie between you and your international counterparts.

Once you have identified these potential differences, what do you *do* about them? Below I offer some general advice on these two dozen scales. For simplicity's sake I have organized my suggestions around the five basic culture scales. The suggestions and comments below are brief starting points intended to give you an initial idea of what to watch for in your interactions with people whose cultural orientation is on the opposite side of the scale from your own. In each case, consider how this general advice applies to your own situation.

Equality versus Hierarchy

If you are dealing with people more focused on equality *than you, the following advice applies:*

Try to find appropriate ways to take initiative on your own and expect others to do so also. This could mean that you have to have less of a hands-on management style and that you sometimes allow employees to complete tasks without heavy intervention from you. Or it could mean that you would be expected to take your own initiative without the benefit of the clear and constant direction you may be used to.

Remember that men and women should be treated in essentially the same way regarding work roles and responsibilities. Do not assume females have less power than their male counterparts.

Informality is more common in equality-focused cultures than in hierarchical ones. Do not be shocked if people put less emphasis on courtesy and protocol than you are accustomed to. If you are accustomed to using titles and formal forms of address, use them but know that you will probably be rather quickly invited to use the informal. Continuing to call someone "Dr. Smith" when he has invited you to call him by his first name may actually make him uncomfortable.

Recognize that roles are flexible and managers can be "team players"; for example, the manager who wears a coat and tie may not be at all reluctant to "get his hands dirty" by demonstrating or working with the product.

In equality-focused cultures, it's possible for people to change their status in life (going from "rags to riches," for example), so you should not expect people's roles (social or economic) to limit their behavior in ways you may be accustomed to. It's important to value (or at least consider) everyone's opinion, point of view, and contribution in equality-focused cultures.

Express your opinions confidently even if you do not have positional power. For example, it's often okay to challenge the opinion of someone leading a meeting. I would not suggest, however, that you go so far as to be brash or to discard diplomacy.

If you are dealing with people more focused on hierarchy *than you, these suggestions apply:*

Recognize that men and women may play distinct social and work roles. Be mindful of the separate sets of expectations or limitations on behavior that apply to men and women in different ways. In many cultures men are generally expected to be more "masculine" and women are expected to be more "feminine" than in equality-focused cultures. The very words *masculine* and *feminine* can upset and confuse people from equality-focused cultures, because they are both ambiguous and emotionally charged. Men are expected to do the driving in many places (or negotiate, pay for the meals, or courteously open the doors), and women place high value on keeping themselves pretty and well-groomed. Since this potentially infuriates American women, often the first advice I give to Americans is to not try to change this aspect of other cultures. Cultures with distinct sex roles are not "thirty years behind the U.S." Rather than changing someone else's entire society, I suggest you learn the different roles people play and honor them within the boundaries of that society.

Some American women traveling overseas to Asia and the Middle East have found they are taken more seriously if they use business cards with an important title when traveling to places where men tend to be the only ones who hold positions of power. For example, an American woman may only be a sales *manager*, but her business card will read *President of Sales*.

Be mindful and respectful of your international counterparts' titles. Pay attention to how people use titles, formality, and protocols, and try to emulate this. Choose to be formal rather than informal. Use formal forms of address until you are invited to use the informal.

Learn which person can accomplish the task you want taken care of. In hierarchies, the manager is expected to be "the boss," and the subordinates are clearly below the boss. People do not easily step outside of their social roles or job functions. If you ask the wrong person to do a job, sometimes he or she takes no action at all.

Follow the proper paths of communication. For example, it may be expected that you include bosses or subordinates in communication. If you're not sure, ask.

In hierarchy-focused cultures, people may not have the same social flexibility or mobility you are accustomed to, but they are more likely to have a clear identity. For example, women may not really have the option of becoming construction workers or changing their own tires, but this does not make them anything less than their counterparts in your culture. Such women may have very clear notions of who they are, and they may struggle less with their identity than American women do. Equivalent comments would apply to men who cannot choose to work as nurses or secretaries as they can in equality-focused cultures. Do not assume that limited social mobility or less flexibility in choosing roles implies a life of unhappiness or restriction the same way it might at home.

Find tactful ways of questioning the opinions of those in power. For instance, you might want to wait until the end of a meeting before challenging what the leader of the meeting is saying. This is especially true of cultures that value face and harmony.

Direct versus Indirect

If you are dealing with people who prefer to be more direct *than you:*

Try to say what you mean concisely and directly. It's usually quite acceptable to say "No" or "I can't" or "It's impossible to have the shipment ready by Tuesday" when those things are true.

Focus more on *what* is said than *how* it is said. This advice might, for example, apply to an Asian dealing with an American; if an American says he is pleased with the product but has to get the approval of his superiors, that is likely exactly what he means. It is probably not an attempt to stall for time, nor is it likely to be a veiled rejection. But I am cautious in making this suggestion, because whenever cultures mix, there is potential for misunderstanding the deeper context of what is said.

Many direct cultures emphasize the written word and contracts. Legal contracts are not merely symbolic, and they don't imply mistrust; they should be treated seriously.

Expect some conflicts to be dealt with much more openly than you may be accustomed to. This should not mean a loss of face for you. People from direct cultures often prefer to "get the issues out on the table" where they can be discussed. Indirectness can be seen as apathy or even dishonesty.

It's difficult to generalize about the rules for talking and the typical flow of conversation, but most direct cultures do not value silence in conversation. To people from indirect cultures silence may mean disagreement or reluctance or simply thoughtful respect, but to people from direct cultures, silence often simply means *nothing*. Taking turns while talking (as Americans do) or interrupting (as Latin Americans do) is more common in direct cultures. Try to communicate what you have to say with words, not nonverbally.

People from direct cultures are often linear thinkers and they may become impatient if you don't quickly get "straight to the point."

If you are dealing with people who prefer to be more indirect *than you:*

Be prepared to use more tact than usual. Be mindful of *how* you say things, not just *what* you say. Also pay attention to what is *not* said, and watch for nonverbal clues. For example, are you perceiving tension and closed body language even while a person is saying "Yes" to you? Then *yes* may not mean *yes*.

Notice and then try to use the formalities, protocols and appropriate diplomatic and respectful language people employ when speaking.

You may need to play a more passive role than you normally do. Be very cautious about raising difficult topics or resolving sensitive issues. Be especially mindful not to be overly direct in situations involving conflict. This is especially true of Asian cultures, where face and harmony are valued. Interrupting a speaker is usually to be avoided, and sometimes it's better to say nothing or delay your response until later if you are not sure how you should react in a certain situation.

Indirect people can be circular thinkers and generally don't like to jump straight to the point. You may need to resist the urge to push the conversation or meeting in order to get your indirect colleagues to state a point directly.

Individual versus Group

If you are dealing with people who have a more individual *focus than you:*

You may need to be more independently resourceful and take individual initiative in new ways. The goal of the team may be the most important, but you may be expected to focus more on your individual performance and what you contribute individually. Voice your opinions assertively in meetings.

Expect to get to know people based on who they are as a unique individual, not based on who their family is or on their work identity.

When working in individually focused cultures, be prepared to be transitioned in and out of teams (or groups or work areas or even different cities) more than you might expect in your own culture. Personal time off can be more important than working long hours or dedication to the company.

In individually focused cultures, command or collaborative decision-making styles are more common than the consensus style. Be prepared to make decisions on your own in situations where you might normally consult with your superior or include your team.

Employees are often motivated by personal incentives and expect to be rewarded similarly. A personal reward for "employee of the month" or "top salesperson" may motivate people more than impersonal group rewards such as "best sales team."

Perhaps ironically, in individualistic cultures it is possible to get closer into someone's space while greeting or speaking than in group-oriented cultures. For example, Americans, Canadians, and Australians greet with handshakes, while the more densely populated Japanese bow without making contact.

The reasoning style of "starting with the conclusion" may be prominent in individually focused cultures. This type of reasoning style is well designed to support opposite views. Consider the United States, which is seen as a land of opposite extremes; religious anti-abortion groups are toward one end of a spectrum and civil liberties groups are toward the other.

If you are dealing with people who are more group *focused than you:*

Be mindful of group goals, group performance, and generally place the group before yourself; remember, your own individual initiative is not the best way to demonstrate your value as an employee.

Expect to spend more time fitting in. Americans often think people from group cultures are "cold" because they don't say, "We ought to get together sometime!" as Americans do so casually. Expect that it may take longer to be fully accepted into a group, but once you are, the affiliation can be quite strong.

Expect decisions, especially consensus decisions, to take more time. This depends on the nature of the decision, and an exception can be companies in hierarchically focused cultures where the person at the top issues a decision that appears to have been made quickly.

While people from individualistic cultures may prefer personalized reward systems, people from group-oriented cultures often feel awkward when singled out like this, because the *team* performance may be more important. One person will not be comfortable taking all the recognition. Find ways to recognize the group's performance, not what an individual has contributed to the group.

Try to conform to social norms and to follow the right protocols. This will be more effective than sticking out as an individual and disregarding conventions. Groups can be very creative, but the process doesn't happen by bucking the conventions of the group itself.

Group cultures typically prefer standardized procedures and guidelines. If the rules apply to one, they may apply to all. But the opposite can also be true: occasionally in group cultures special exceptions may be made for people such as hired relatives.

Consensus or collaborative decision-making styles are common. Be prepared to incorporate others more and to move more slowly through the decision-making process as a result.

The reasoning style of "arriving at the conclusion all at once" may occur in group-oriented cultures (such as in Asia), where many people are consulted during a consensus or collaborative decision-making process.

In some group cultures (such as densely populated Asian cultures), people may prefer more physical distance and less physical contact than you might expect or than you might be accustomed to. In other group-oriented societies, however (for example, most South American cultures), people stand close while speaking and touch each other frequently. An exception to the Asian distance rule is the Japanese practice of pushing and packing people into subway trains.

Task versus Relationship

If you are dealing with people who are more task *focused than you:*

Expect things to move rather rapidly. Work relationships can form quickly for the purpose of accomplishing the task at hand. They can then dissolve equally quickly when the team disbands or when the project is finished. Do not be surprised when someone you've only just met thrusts a business card into your hand and proposes collaboration. These people may be trying to seize the opportunity of meeting you; they should not be dismissed as being insincere.

People will initially want to know you based on what you *do*, not who you *are*. It may seem ironic given the fact that work relationships can form so quickly, but yet some people won't want to share personal information with you about themselves.

Task-focused people can be very career oriented and put energy into their work, and are known for long work hours and very little vacation time. But because they can also clearly distinguish between work time and time off, they highly value time away from work. They may "live to work," but employees from task-focused cultures do have a life and other priorities outside of work.

If there's a job to be done, you may be expected to take the initiative, especially in cultures with an individual focus. For example, when you are in Canada or the United States, be prepared to be a self-starter and get straight to work. If you don't understand what is expected of you, you cannot simply fail to take action. You must instead do what is necessary to clarify what the expectations are.

When people from task-focused cultures use a very linear communication style that gets straight to the point, this does not mean they are not interested in you personally. Their first priority is on accomplishing the task at hand: "Business before pleasure."

Time is often seen as scarce in task-focused cultures, and you may have to adjust to a quicker pace of life.

Quality in a task-focused culture may simply mean "Does it do the job?" rather than "Is it aesthetically pleasing?"

If you are dealing with people who are more relationship *focused than you:*

Plan extra time for initiating and nurturing professional relationships. Don't make the typically American mistake of hoping to close an important deal halfway around the world on a three-day trip.

Learn the protocols used for maintaining professional relationships, such as use of polite language, proper introductions, acknowledging others, and spending time maintaining good relations rather than simply getting straight to work. The process of working together sometimes matters more than the result.

Do not expect employees to make sacrifices such as working weekends. People from relationship-focused cultures will sometimes *work to live* rather than *live to work*. Mexico is an example of a country that is relationship focused and where people work to live. This does not mean that Mexicans are lazy; they are indeed very industrious. Japan represents a surprising mix on this issue: the Japanese expect you to work hard at nurturing relationships, yet they also *live to work*. So, although there are exceptions, the general rule is that people from relationship-focused cultures will not tend to make drastic sacrifices for work.

Make tasks and procedures as clear as possible if you expect them to be completed or followed. Recall my American client who delighted his Japanese partners by posting a Web page of shipping requirements and procedures (from required paperwork to the payment process).

People from relationship-focused cultures will often follow a circular or zigzag communication style instead of getting straight to the point. Recognize that the tangents and loops involved in these styles are much more than unnecessary distractions; they are an important way of verifying and enhancing the work relationship. Pay attention to subtle, indirect statements of the point.

Similarly, people from relationship-focused cultures may not be comfortable sticking to just one task at a time. Multitasking often involves nurturing the work relationship, while accomplishing job goals.

You may have to adjust to a slower pace of life because the most important goal, rather than jumping straight to the task at hand, is often building proper working relationships, and this takes time.

Recognize that quality may not be defined in ways you are accustomed to. Rather than merely asking whether a product does the job, often significant weight can be given to other factors such as aesthetics and beauty.

Risk versus Caution

If you are dealing with people who are more comfortable with risk *than you:*

Be prepared to move quickly in business and professional life.

The focus is often on the present and the very near future. Business plans cover the next few quarters or years, not the next twenty or fifty years. Learn to be comfortable with last-minute changes; they are often acceptable and desirable.

Decisions can be made quickly and with little information. Because decisions are made quickly, the implementation process necessarily moves more slowly.

The view of people comfortable with risk is that risks are usually informed and calculated risks, certainly not stupid gambles. Calculated risks imply a level of control over life and business; you may need to raise your comfort level with such risks.

Expect fewer rules, regulations, guidelines, and directions. Innovations and risk go hand in hand in these cultures.

If you are dealing with people who are more comfortable with caution *than you:*

While innovations may occur less frequently in caution-oriented cultures than in risk-oriented ones, wonderful refinements are often mainstays of caution-oriented cultures. Consider the Japanese Walkman as an example of continued refinement in precision engineering and design. The Japanese may not be creative inventors, but they are masterful manufacturers. You may need to find new ways of defining continual improvement and creativity. One of those ways involves sticking to the proven path rather than innovating with spontaneous methods. Lateral thinking may involve novel combinations using past precedents rather than brand-new ideas.

New initiatives may require more patience. While decision making may proceed slowly, implementation can happen quite quickly, properly, and efficiently once the decision has been made. Focus on the long-term consequences in the decisions you are involved with.

Some people may be cautious and avoid risks because they don't feel a high level of control over business or life. Focus on how you can help such people take reasonable and calculated risks in business.

The focus can be more on past precedents of what worked and what didn't. Expect to engage in more preparation, more background work, more research, and to use more hindsight as you move forward.

The reasoning style of working toward the conclusion necessarily involves careful study and patience. You may need to curb your desire for instant gratification and quick decisions.

Do not expect to change plans at the last minute. Just "tossing out an idea" when the decision has been made or has almost been made can disorient those who prefer caution.

Communication Skills

I believe most readers of this book will be speaking English as they interact with international colleagues and encounter differences based on the five basic culture scales above. Americans enjoy the luxury of being able to communicate with much of the rest of the world without having to learn a single word of another language. This is indeed a privilege. English is a difficult language to learn, and native English speakers are fortunate that (1) they learned the language fluently without much conscious effort and (2) nonnative English speakers have put great effort into learning to speak English.

Consider this as illustration of how difficult English is: If *through* is pronounced "throo," then *plough* should be "ploo," but it's "plow." *Cough* might then be "cow," not "coff." But then *enough* could be "enoff," not "enuff," and *dough* should then be "duff," right? English pronunciation is wildly variable, compared with many languages.

It's also very tricky to learn which syllable gets the accent in English words: beginning, (ARKansas), middle (alaBAMa), or end (deTROIT). Other languages, such as French, balance words so that instead of piAno, as in English, the accents are equal: "pi-a-no" (in French). Spanish and Portuguese at least have accents over the letters that are stressed; English doesn't.

We are perhaps fortunate to not have the confusion of masculine or feminine (or neutral!) nouns in English, as many other languages do. In Portuguese, for example, a house is "feminine," but a book is "masculine," and in German a girl is "neutral!"

Japanese forms singular and plural differently (one book, two book, three book), and so English plurals with the added *s* can be difficult for the Japanese. English plurals, though, contain many exceptions. Why does *mouse* or *moose* not become "mices" or "mooses"? Why does *tooth* become *teeth* but "booth" not become "beeth"?

There are scores of books dedicated to the intricacies of English spelling and grammar, but this is not my purpose, so I will end by repeating my earlier point that native English speakers are very fortunate to have learned the basic rules without much conscious effort. Because English is a global language, the rest of the world has done—and continues to do—its best to communicate intelligibly in that language.

Since you are the lucky ones because you are already fluent in English (or you wouldn't be reading this book), I'm going to propose that you try your hardest to use the clearest English possible when speaking with nonfluent English speakers. Below are ten tips for doing this.

Ten Tips for Making the Most of Your English

One of the ways we establish relationships in any language, whether working relationships or friendships, is through "familiar" language. For example, two people who are beginning to work together might get comfortable and use a bit of idiomatic or relaxed language in their speech. One might say, "Okay Ivan, let me run another idea past you...." Admittedly, this sounds less cold and formal than saying, "Now, Ivan, there is another idea I would like to talk about." But relaxed speech can be confusing and alienating to nonnative speakers.

If you've ever gone through the (enriching and highly recommended) experience of studying another language, you probably also learned a lot about English as you tried translating your thoughts into the second language. Here's an example. If you speak another language, ask yourself how you'd say *get* in that language. There is no equivalent to the English *get* in any of the several languages I speak at least partially. Expressions with *get* are also hard to translate. Do you mean *get* in the sense of "become lost" (get lost), "understand" (get the main point), "leave" (get out of here), "start" (get going), "continue" (get on with the meeting), or "purchase" (get some supplies at the store)? With nonnative English speakers, it's better to use more precise verbs to describe what you're actually "getting at" (explaining).

If you want to be precise and avoid confusion, I propose using "international business English" when you are dealing with nonnative English speakers; that is, clear, articulate, and simple English that is free of slang, "relaxed expressions," idioms, and complex grammatical constructions. Here are ten specific tips to help you communicate more clearly in English (or any language).

Tip 1: *Avoid sports and military idiomatic expressions.* Our language is permeated with such expressions. Try putting these following into international business English:

- We need a level playing field.
- This project is a strikeout.
- Let me run this idea past you.
- That plan has been sidelined.
- Am I in the ballpark?
- We're dealing with a "snafu" here.
- Joe really shoots from the hip.
- Fire off a memo to Christine.
- There is no magic bullet.

See page 218 for some possible ways of changing these examples into clear English.

Tip 2: *Keep it simple.* Sometimes in an effort to speak properly or clearly, people choose words such as *utilize* instead of *use*. When you do this, you're going in the wrong direction by making things more confusing for nonnative speakers. You might be haunted by the image of past English teachers who encouraged you to learn and use bigger and more impressive words, but with speakers who have limited English proficiency, use basics such as *put, take,* or *more* instead of *position, remove,* or *additional.* In spite of the many meanings of *get* shown above, if the word "gets" you there, go for it![†]

Where the "keep it simple" tip applies most is with entire sentences. Try to avoid run-on sentences. Especially when the listener has very low English proficiency, you might want to speak in shorter sentences (but not insultingly) and give the person adequate time to absorb what you say instead of rambling on into more complex ideas.

---

† On the other hand, some people propose that longer English words (such as *utilize*) can be better than shorter ones because they can give speakers of some other languages a better chance of recognizing a similar word in their language. *Put* is shorter than *position* (as in, "Position this graphic on the middle of the page please"), but *position* would be more recognizable to a French speaker because the French use the exact same word—*position*—but don't use anything like *put* in this sense. In some cases, speakers of Germanic languages (German, Scandinavian languages) or Latin-based languages (French, Spanish, Italian, Portuguese) might be able to better recognize longer words.

Tip 3: *Give and seek feedback.* Even if you send the message in clear, simple English, you can't be certain there has been communication until the receiver acknowledges it with feedback. So, ask for feedback often (but not after every sentence!) to make sure your listener is understanding what you intend to communicate.

There are two kinds of questions you can use when seeking feedback:

1. Closed-ended questions: These usually begin with *do, did, does, is, are, will,* or *can.* These questions can be answered with a simple yes or no (or maybe an "uh-huh" or a "uh-uh"). However, I recommend that you avoid closed-ended questions, because people will frequently simply say yes even if they don't understand you. This is especially true of people who believe in saving face for the speaker or in being indirect. If someone doesn't want to offend you or doesn't want to directly confront you on something, he may simply say or nod yes.

2. Open-ended questions: These usually begin with *who, what, why, where, when, how,* or *how many.* This is the better choice, because it's not possible to answer these questions with a grunt or a simple yes. For example, you can't answer the question "How do you think we should do this plan?" without revealing whether you have understood. As you might guess, it can be difficult to get feedback from those who prefer to be indirect or save face because of their cultural programming.

Remember, in addition to asking for feedback, you will sometimes do well to offer it.

Here's a perspective to remember when it comes to speaking your language with nonnative speakers: when people don't understand you, you might know it because

There's a big difference between misunderstanding and not understanding!

the conversation may stop and you may not be able to get what you want. But when people *mis*understand you, you probably won't know it because they probably won't tell you. They may or may not give you a strange look, which you may or may not notice, but in these cases the conversation can go on...under a few false assumptions.

Here's an example. Imagine I am trying to tell someone, "I want to help you." If she doesn't understand, she may ask me to repeat. But if, because of the similarity of the words *want* and *won't* she understands me to be saying "I *won't* help you," she may be puzzled but may just file that in her memory bank and continue the conversation—under the misconception that you aren't a very giving person. As I noted in Part 5, *mis*understandings are inherently problematic because by their very nature they go unnoticed.

Tip 4: *Speak slowly and clearly—but not loudly*. This rule is simple. Be sure not to speak insultingly slowly, and be sure not to shout. I recommend to Americans that they be careful to not portray arrogance and that they avoid condescension at all costs. Often when people don't speak our language, we seem to treat them as though they are deaf or even worse, "slow." Never assume lesser intelligence just because someone does not speak your native language. Just remember to speak clearly, and instead of asking "Tcha-gonna-do-'bout-th'-invoice?" ask more slowly and articulately, "What are you going to do about the invoice?"

Tip 5: *Repeat if necessary*. Listening in a foreign language can be exhausting, and it's possible to "get behind" or simply not hear a word one knows. Think about how you "fill in the blanks" when you listen to songs. You don't hear every word of the lyrics, but you usually hear enough to guess what word goes in the blank. However, the "surrounding sounds" (or context) of the sentence might not help a limited-English speaker, so you may simply need to repeat something.

What word goes into the blank here: "I left you a message on your _____"? Because you've heard this in English countless times, you can easily plug the phrase "answering machine" or "voice mail" in the blank. Even if I say this and mumble the last words, you will still "hear" them.

Tip 6: *Use precise language*. Familiar expressions such as "take the bus" or "catch the bus" can be confusing. No humans (or dogs!) I know are fast enough to actually *catch* a moving bus. And is it the bus that "takes" us or do we "take" it? To say "ride" the bus may be clearer. If these are confusing, what we call two-word verbs are a nightmare for English learners.

Think about the confusion that might result if you used the two-word verb from Tip 1: to "run (something) past (someone)." Or consider the things a nonnative English speaker might imagine when you say, I'll "pick you up at 8 A.M." (Will you use straps or a hoist?) And how high up will they be when you "drop them off" after the meeting? (Should they bring a parachute or just a light crash

Overheard in a taxi: *"Okay Driver! Ready when you are for the drop-off!"*

helmet?) When you are dealing with nonnative English speakers, a clearer way of saying all this could be, "I will come for you at your hotel at 8:00 in the morning and bring you, in my car, to our meeting. After the meeting, I will bring you back to the hotel." To a native speaker this seems tedious, but it's better to be clear than confusing when people do not speak English confidently or understand it well.

I also recommend that you use precise and clear language instead of using proverbs; "A bird in the hand is worth two in the bush" could be quite confusing. Instead, you might say something specific like "We need to work on the Schwartz account right now instead of trying to develop new business." The nonnative speakers you deal with will certainly appreciate your efforts!

Tip 7: *Use clear and common gestures.* Yes, you may have heard that making the American "A-okay" symbol by making a circle with your index finger and your thumb is, in Brazil, the derogatory equivalent of "giving someone the finger." To some, this very same gesture means "zero." I'm sure that somewhere in the world, the gesture of scratching your eyebrow the wrong way might horribly offend someone. What I am suggesting is that you can sometimes support an idea with a clear, impromptu gesture. Do you want a receipt? Make your hands like you are holding one. Do you want to see the book? Open and close your hands as though you are handling a book. Do you want to know the time? Point to your wrist. Don't try to be a mime, just support your words with some obvious body language. It usually works.

Tip 8: *Write it down*. This one is simple. Written material can be taken away and read at a leisurely pace without pressure. Just seeing your message in writing may do the trick, particularly because many English learners are exposed largely to reading and have little chance to practice conversation. If that doesn't work, perhaps someone else at home or back at the office can help translate something that is written.

Tip 9: *Offer examples*. Examples help to support an idea. Here is an example of a typical misunderstanding I have had with limited-English speakers, and variations I have used to find the information I want:

> **Brooks:** Where did you go in Canada?
>
> **Nonnative speaker:** Yes.
>
> **Brooks:** Where did you go in Canada?
>
> **Nonnative speaker:** Ah! Yes! Two weeks.
>
> **Brooks:** What cities did you visit in Canada? Toronto? Montreal? Ottawa?
>
> **Nonnative speaker:** Ottawa, yes, and Victoria!

Now I finally had my answer—but not until I gave an example in the question.

Tip 10: *Summarize*. You can sometimes even ask for summaries of what you have just discussed, but be careful with this one. You can easily offend someone if your tone sounds like you're asking a young child to summarize what you just said. You can summarize in both directions, of course. That is, ask for summaries as feedback, and offer summaries for clarity.

Tip 10½ (free bonus tip): *Take it easy*. Don't take offense if you are asked to slow down, if you have to repeat yourself, or if you can't get your point across. It's not a personal criticism! Remember that by speaking your language, your international partners are already going more than halfway to communicating effectively. And never forget that your counterparts are at least as intelligent as you are—after all, can you speak their language?

Learn to Speak a Relevant Foreign Language

There's a commonly known joke that goes

> **Q:** What do you call a person who speaks three languages?
>
> **A:** Trilingual.
>
> **Q:** What do you call a person who speaks two languages?
>
> **A:** Bilingual.
>
> **Q:** What do you call a person who speaks one language?
>
> **A:** American.

This joke is well-known for good reason. Americans deserve their reputation for being monolinguals, but I don't point a shaming finger at Americans; we can forgive ourselves for being monolinguals if we consider how geographically isolated North America is compared with European countries. A Parisian can travel a few hours in almost any direction and be surrounded by a variety of different languages. A Chicagoan can't really do this in the same way.

Other languages, however, are coming to the Chicagoan! This is true in New York City, Los Angeles, and, yes, even Des Moines. This trend is clearly not going to stop, so Americans are going to have to be involved more and more with other languages, especially Spanish. Because of this trend, I hope children will have wider choices for learning foreign languages so that America will eventually become less monolingual.

American kids can learn languages, but you're probably not a kid reading this book, so should you give up hope? I admit that if you start learning a foreign language when you're a child, you have a much better chance of speaking it fluently and with an appropriate accent. But don't use this as an excuse for not starting as an adult. I firmly believe that you can increase your capacity at any age. Because I learned French to native fluency as a kid, I had a head start with languages in general. That head start made it pretty easy to learn survival Spanish in college, and I have since been able to bring my Portuguese to a level of conversational proficiency.

You can rest assured, though, that I will likely *never* have much proficiency in Chinese, Japanese, Arabic, Russian, Polish, or many other wonderful languages that are completely different from English or the Latin-based languages. The average Japanese five-year-old can write more Japanese than I ever will, but I don't let this discourage me! While there could never be enough years to learn the languages I want, I still try to learn a bit of each language that is relevant to me. At the moment, I'm spending a bit of time in East Asia, and Mandarin will be especially relevant if I want to eat, travel, enjoy myself, and interact with others.

I can make the locals laugh at my attempts in a few other languages, such as Swedish, but I'm certainly not like the average European who seems to speak "eleventeen" languages. I don't propose to try to achieve that, and you don't need to either. But my Swedish friend, who speaks seven languages, correctly points out that languages are not learned "overnight," and he is always trying to improve his skills in the various languages he speaks.

Speaking a foreign language opens doors for businesspeople. Not doing so is not only a business disadvantage but a social one as well. At the simplest level, going to another country and not speaking the language is a bit like going to summer camp and not knowing how to swim; you can only stand on the dry beach and watch the other kids have a delightful time playing in the water. Because I'm a gregarious person, I love to interact with people, and it's frustrating to not even be able to greet a waiter. When I can't speak the local language, I feel that my personality suffers a tremendous impediment.

More important than not being able to greet waiters, I am unable to express my personality and style the way I can in my native tongue. I can't use humor or *connect* with people in my usual ways. I have found that when I speak French or Portuguese, I actually take on a different personality. My humor and communication patterns necessarily change based on the language I am speaking.

Taking on a foreign name, as many students do in foreign language classes, enhances this new personality. When I learned French as a schoolchild, I became *Hamidou*, not *Brooks*. Hamidou is a traditional Senegalese name, and using it opened a new personality for me simply because I was playing a role (and speaking a corresponding language) outside of my usual patterns. One positive effect of this "role-playing" attitude is that it may make the second-language learner less inhibited, more open to make mistakes, and thereby a better learner.

I don't recommend you go so far as to actually use a different name with your international counterparts, but if they give you a nickname (such as *Steve-san* or *Señor Martin*), enjoy it. More important, be aware of how your personality changes when you speak foreign languages, and enjoy the process. Doing this may help you set some of your ego aside even if you don't speak flawlessly.

I hope this encourages you to learn at least something of a second language. If you can't connect with someone at the most basic conversational level, how can you possibly hope to have any close business connection? Imagine going to Poland with the eventual goal of securing a contract; competitors will be there vying for the contract, too. All other things being equal, you don't stand much of a chance of landing the contract if you're competing with someone who speaks even a little Polish, if you speak none. It would be like trying to impress someone with your dancing when Fred Astaire shows up. I am amazed how many companies don't recognize the whoppingly sound strategy of using employees who speak the native language. Companies should recruit, charm, romance, highly compensate, and do everything else possible to retain employees who have strong second-language skills.

You may or may not be in a position to decide your company's strategy regarding hiring employees who speak the target language fluently, but you can personally decide to increase your own second-language skills. The real business decisions may or may not happen "on the golf course"

> **Take language lessons, not golf lessons, if you really want to do international business with the big players.**

or at the country club, but I wouldn't waste a minute on a golf lesson until I had finished my language classes. You will find your hosts to be far more impressed by someone who has dedicated years to learning another language than to someone who can average par on a golf course.

Fluency Is Not Required

Let's face it; if you are an adult English speaker and you have never studied Mandarin Chinese, you stand very little chance of ever speaking it with native fluency. Eastern languages, which use characters different from the twenty-six letters of the English alphabet, are very tough for Westerners to learn, regardless of age.

If Chinese, Japanese, Korean, or Arabic are "10" on the difficulty scale for English speakers, Russian might be a "6" or "7," French might be a "3" or "4" and Spanish, a "1." Give yourself a break with some of the more difficult languages, and don't worry if you don't achieve anything close to fluency.

No matter what language you are trying to learn, first take the pressure off yourself and set a reasonable goal. Passable conversational fluency is certainly commendable. I hope you take that comment as reassurance, not as discouragement, because even as an adult, you can learn enough for everyday basic communication.

By basic communication skill I mean, for example, can you have a casual conversation with someone? Can you ask for a bigger box, inquire about what city a bus goes to, find the location of a building? Can you talk about the weather or compliment your host? Can you ask for and understand directions to the train station? If you can attain this level of conversational proficiency, you will have a wonderful advantage when traveling or when interacting with people from different places.

Learn the Six Basics

If you're heading to or dealing with people from a major city in most parts of the world, you will probably have the luxury of being able to communicate in English. If you are interacting with people from other cultures in your own country, you will almost certainly be using English.

But even if you *can* get by most of the time speaking English and if you absolutely don't have the time to study the most relevant language to the degree of conversational proficiency, at least show a bare minimum of respect for and courtesy to your hosts by learning what I call the "six basics" of their language.

1. Yes.

2. No.

3. Please.

4. Thank you.

5. Hello.

6. Good-bye.

Don't board a plane for a foreign country without knowing these expressions in the language of the place you're going to! Using them can be an easy way to charm people. I once said to a visiting Korean, *"Kam saham nida"* (of course Koreans don't spell it with Western letters that way). The phrase I am trying to spell out for you means "thank you" in Korean. Apparently, I pronounced it passably (or she was being polite and saving the bumbling American's face), because she said in English, "Oh! You speak Korean very well!" Naturally I could only tell her *"Kam saham nida"* in reply to this because "thank you" happened to be the only bit I knew in Korean at the time! Sometimes just one well-placed word or expression in someone's native language can help make a good impression.

Even if you have very limited language proficiency, pay attention to nonverbal "language"; watch how close people stand to each other, whether they touch each other occasionally during conversation. Observe eye contact, posture, politeness, and so on. Nonverbal behaviors make up much of how people communicate, and you can really make a bad impression if you get these wrong. Conversely, becoming familiar with your host culture's nonverbal behavior will help you make a positive first impression.

There are numerous language guidebooks and multitudes of approaches for learning languages. I started teaching French to kids at language immersion summer camps when I was sixteen years old and have taught all the way up to advanced business French for MBA students. Naturally, I've seen a lot of language textbooks—some good and some really horrible. The phonetic (fon-etik) pronunciation guides in language books and dictionaries are at best only rough representations of how something sounds. At worst, they are flat out *wrong*. Never rely on a written guide alone. Written materials accompanied by tapes are useful, but the best method is to have a native speaker coach you through the pronunciation of the words and phrases (it often helps to see a person's lips as you are learning).

[man-ee fonetik gides ar not vary gud.]

Also remember that the six words and phrases are indeed very basic. For example, no matter what the language, there are different ways of saying "hello" based on the situation (the time of day, how well you know the person, if it's over the phone or face-to-face, etc.). Work on building your vocabulary and practice speaking as much as you can with your limited means.

Pay Attention to the Formalities and Protocols

Many languages distinguish between a formal and an informal way of saying things. In French, for example, *tu* (you) is used for close friends and children, and *vous* (also "you") is used for adult acquaintances, for strangers, and when speaking to more than one person. *Vous* shows respect. If you are speaking English, say, in Germany, the same distinction applies. Also, use the person's title (Mr., Mrs., Ms., Dr.) and last name.

Another recommendation: Speakers of Spanish, Portuguese, French, Italian, German, and other languages sometimes like to add "miss," "madam," or "sir" at the end of a sentence or expression to show respect ("Thank you, sir"). Again, pay attention to how the locals do this. You can charm people (instead of putting them off) by using a title of respect like this.

Watch for other things as well. For example, you might take it for granted that in the United States cashiers say "Thank you," and you respond "Thank you. Good-bye." We seem to say "Thank you" for almost anything in the U.S.; I once muttered "Thank you" as the police officer who had just given me a speeding ticket turned to walk back to his car. In France when cashiers say "Thank you," you merely say "Good-bye." This is because the cashier has thanked you for the business and the French feel there's no need to echo "thank you" back at them. The French think it's a bit weird to thank a cashier. I had to unlearn my tendency to thank everyone when I was in front of French cashiers.

In addition to learning *how* to say "hello" as one of the six basics, pay attention to *when* people use greetings and whether their greetings include more elements than "hello": questions about family, health, even whether both conversants have eaten yet (China) or slept well (morning greeting in Hausa). In my daily life in France, there were about 30 people I had to stop and greet the first time I saw them on any given day. To not say hello (accompanied by a handshake for men or a kiss on each cheek for women) would have been rude. Recall my example in Part 4 of the Frenchman who offered his elbow to a colleague when his arms were so full of books he couldn't shake hands. An American would have been satisfied with a nod of the head and/or a "hey," but the Frenchman went to lengths to complete the greeting. Greetings are just one of many examples you may encounter of how people use language in specific ways within their daily routines. Pay attention to what language is used in a variety of situations; answering the phone, at meals, interrupting someone, and so forth—to the extent, of course, of your language skills.

The general advice I give regarding formalities and protocol is that it's better to be overly polite than discourteous. Perhaps partly because of my culture and partly because of my personality, I am accustomed to informality. I started teaching as a professor in my early thirties and used to insist that students call me by my first name. Foreign students would usually start by calling me Dr. Peterson or Professor Peterson (not unlike the Japanese letter writer in Part 1). Early on, I would insist that students call me Brooks. Although some international students adjusted to this, others apparently never felt comfortable using my first name. Now I let the students use these formalities with me if they wish—even "Dr. Brooks."

Be a Sympathetic Native Listener

When I was a graduate student, I taught undergraduate French classes, as did most of the students who were pursuing their master's in French. At the end of each semester, part of our teaching duties involved conducting interviews for the "Graduation Proficiency Test." This was the French speaking test students needed to pass in order to complete their college studies, and many were terrified of it.

The students taking the test didn't know it, but we were instructed to conduct the interviews as "sympathetic native listeners." What that meant was, if someone didn't say something *exactly* like a French person would say it, we were not supposed to throw up our hands or shrug our shoulders and give a confused "Pardon?" as if we had no idea what the person had said. Instead, we were instructed to consider whether a native French speaker who did not understand English (but who was a sympathetic listener) would understand what the student had said.

This concept has been useful to me in various international settings, and you can use it in two ways: (1) you can be a sympathetic native listener, and (2) you can encourage those to whom you talk to be sympathetic native listeners, too. Here are two real stories illustrating how each might work.

A South American friend was going through the checkout lane at a large department store in the United States. When the time came to pay, he extended an American Express card to the cashier and asked, "Do you get American Express?" The cashier gave a blank look as if the man had just asked, *"Zorg skibbet schnokker knilk?"* The South American man asked again, "Do you get American Express?" which drew another *completely* blank look from the cashier. Apparently, the total communication breakdown came from the word *get*. This South American man was well educated and spoke English proficiently, but because he was not a native English speaker, he sometimes forgot or didn't know the right idiomatic usage: "Do you *take* American Express?"

The clues should have been obvious: This interaction is happening at a checkout counter, and the client is extending an American Express card. Actually, with all these clues the cashier should have been able to understand the South American's question, even if he had said, *"Zorg skibbet schnokker knilk American Express?"*

The cashier in this scenario could easily have been a more sympathetic native listener. I try to keep that in mind when I hear someone speaking to me with a Hindi or German accent. I get ready to creatively listen *around* as many words as I can.

The second story happened the first time I went to Taiwan. I had taken a bus from the small city of Hsinchu to Taipei. Nearly all buses in my area ran on one road and practically all of them went to Taipei, so getting there was easy. Returning, however, was a different story. The Taipei central bus station had about a dozen departure gates, and Hsinchu was not the destination of most of the buses.

Zorg skibbet schnokker knilk American Express?

So, speaking in my extremely limited Chinese and relying heavily on the word *Hsinchu*, I was directed to board what I thought was the right bus. As I got on the bus, I raised my eyebrows and asked the driver "Hsinchu?" He tore the corner off my ticket, as they usually do when you board but did not communicate *anything* to me (verbally or nonverbally). "Hsinchu?" I asked again, pointing at this bus, and indicating out the front window where it was headed. Again there was absolutely no response from the driver. There were several people waiting behind me…so I boarded the bus.

I had indeed been on the right bus to Hsinchu, and I obviously survived to tell this story. What I learned was this strategy: in the future, I would *not* hand the driver my ticket to tear until I got a response from him. This was a pretty easy communication situation because I was giving the driver all the clues, and even if the driver couldn't speak a word of English and I only spoke a few words of Chinese, the driver definitely would know the "thumbs up" gesture, a *very* common one in Taiwan.

By withholding the ticket, I would "help" the driver to be a sympathetic native listener! He *had* to work with me. This is admittedly a bold thing to do when you are a stranger in someone else's country, so I was always very polite. Taiwanese bus drivers are not necessarily skilled cross-cultural communication experts; nor are they friendly to strangers.

These stories are examples describing two ordinary situations. When you're faced with language barriers, I encourage you to find ways in which you can listen sympathetically and also to find ways in which you can effectively encourage others to do the same—without losing your temper.

A Word on Using Translators and Interpreters

In some instances, being a sympathetic native listener (or encouraging others to do so) will not be enough. Sometimes conversational proficiency will not be enough for you to communicate what you need to say. Sometimes the language barriers will be too great or the level of precision, detail, or importance of the communication too high for you to communicate on your own. In these cases, you will need to use a translator or an interpreter. Many of us confuse the terms *translation* and *interpretation*, so let's set that straight before going any further. *Translation* refers to the written word, and *interpretation* refers to the spoken word. Choosing competent translators and interpreters can be difficult; I will try to give you some helpful points to keep in mind.

Translators

Clients sometimes ask me for recommendations for decent translation software that can handle their marketing materials. The short answer is that there is none. Computers have brought us tremendous advances in communication, but when it comes to language translation programs, beware!

Take a simple sentence such as "There were a lot of fans in the stadium." A free software translation program on the Web came up with this French sentence: *"Il y avait beaucoup de ventilateurs dans le stade."* Back-translated into English, that makes the ridiculous statement, "There were a lot of fans (breeze blowing, ventilation type) in the stadium."

Fan is a simple word that means both "spectator" and "wind maker." More complicated are words such as *just*, which can mean "recently" (I just arrived), "only" (It's just me), "fair" (Her decision was just), "simply" (Just dial 1-800...), "really" (I just can't believe it!), "exclusively" (This offer is just available on Friday), and so on.

Computers certainly aren't alone in making costly and embarrassing translation mistakes; people make them, too. Entire books detail translation gaffes that companies have made.

I enjoy looking for English mistranslations in slogans on scooters in Asia. Reading them on the hundreds of scooters parked along the sidewalks always makes me chuckle. Here are four of my favorites:

- The Epochal Scooter. (Are they trying to say "The scooter of the times"? "The unparalleled scooter"?)

- We reach for the sky. Neither does civilization. (Your guess is as good as mine what the second part of this one means.)

- The best function and good sensation. (No comment.)

- The scooter of wind called 125. (Must be a speedy one!)

I think these are good illustrations of why it's important to use a trained translator. The idea intended by the company often does come across in the scooter slogans, but the improper phrasing can make it look silly. Slogans such as these could have been corrected or improved by a skilled translator in under a minute. One single fax, e-mail, or phone call could have cleared the problem up, before scooters appeared on the streets by the thousands.

Successful translation must also respect cultural style. For example, as I mentioned in Part 4 in the story of the advertising piece on French handbags, the French tend to use very long, even poetic, product descriptions in their advertising. French advertisers may attempt to appeal to the customers' sense of logic, reason, and good taste. Americans, in contrast, promote product features in short, bullet-point lists that will grab the customer's eye. Neither style will be successful in the other country if the translator isn't sensitive to these different styles.

In summary, the cost of hiring an experienced translator is a small price to pay to avoid embarrassment to your company, its product image, and you (face).

More than just using highly qualified native translators, I cannot encourage companies strongly enough to use *local* foreign ad agencies when introducing products or services to those foreign markets abroad. When targeting a local client or customer of a particular cultural background, make sure your approach respects and effectively taps into that person's culture.

Interpreters

Hiring and working with an interpreter involves a specific set of considerations that include and even go beyond those of working with translators.

Interpreters must, of course, have all the highly honed language skills of translators. But unlike translators, interpreters are more "on the spot" because they are performing "live." Interpreters don't have the luxury of pausing to consult a dictionary or going off to stretch and have a cup of tea while they are working.

There are also social or psychological considerations inherent in working with interpreters because they are speaking by your side and, in a sense, on your behalf. If you express annoyance or delight in your tone of voice, should the interpreter show this through his or her tone of voice also? No, this can be distracting or, worse, destructive to the conversation. Can the interpreter refrain from taking sides and maintain accuracy and objectivity as a heated discussion unfolds? Hopefully! Interpreters should be impartial and not take sides, especially not in a way that undermines your position. This could be a risk when you use an interpreter provided by your international counterpart.

Interpreters should not overly dramatize what you are saying. If you have a certain tone of voice while you speak, your international counterpart will certainly hear it; the interpreter doesn't need to mimic. Good interpreters will not do this. If you see this happening, I suggest you tactfully bring it to the interpreter's attention during a break.

Make sure you always speak for yourself and never let the interpreter answer a question for you. Even if the interpreter knows the answer to the question you were asked, you should answer. I faced this problem when I was teaching a graduate-school course through an interpreter I had worked with on the same course before. She was familiar with the material and could perhaps have answered some questions on her own, but because she respected my role as professor and was a good interpreter, she stayed within her role and allowed me to stay within mine. You should *never* be left a passive observer as your international counterparts carry on a conversation with the interpreter.

At the same time, it is very useful—and sometimes essential—that the interpreter have sufficient knowledge of the material being discussed. Interpreters in any industry should have some knowledge of that industry. For example, medical interpreters need to know medical terms. No matter how good the interpreter, though, you are ultimately responsible for successful communication. Below are some guidelines that I have found to be particularly helpful.

1. While speaking through an interpreter, engage your counterpart directly. Even if you can't understand what your counterpart is saying, look at her while she is speaking and while you are speaking to her. *Do not* merely turn and face the interpreter while you converse. I am not suggesting you pretend to understand someone who is speaking Russian to you but rather that you show you are interested and tuned in to your counterpart's body language by engaging with her as she speaks. After all, you can study body language and listen for tone of voice. So be sure to respectfully connect with your counterpart in spite of the language barrier.

2. Plan carefully before the interpreted conversation is to take place. You'll need additional time. I find it takes me about twice as long as usual to give a presentation and lead activities when working with an interpreter. Expect the interpreter to be able to handle a few sentences at a time. Typically, you will speak a few sentences, the interpreter translates, your counterpart(s) responds, the interpreter translates those remarks back to you, and so forth. ("Simultaneous interpretation" is when neither speaker pauses and the interpreter translates with a slight delay behind the speaker. This type of interpretation is usually reserved for settings such as United Nations meetings, very large presentations, and so forth.)

3. You may also find that you need to restructure activities. For example, I have learned that brainstorming doesn't work because I can't instantaneously understand what several people are quickly suggesting. (And incidentally, many other cultures are not as comfortable with brainstorming as Americans are.) Similarly, if I am leading a group in the United States, I can break them into smaller groups for discussion while I circulate around the room listening to each group. I might then present a summary of some of the most relevant points I overheard. With an interpreter at my side, I feel more encumbered, the process is not as effective, and spontaneity is lost.

4. Avoid humor with presentations. Americans typically start almost any meeting or presentation with a "chuckler," such as "I'm glad to be here...especially after tromping through those mountains of snow on the way in!" (...and the audience chuckles...). This ever-present chuckler is intended to put both the audience and speaker at ease and as such is effective—for American audiences. But few other countries practice this custom. It can lead to even more awkward situations when attempted through an interpreter. Remember, humor has been said to be the hardest thing to grasp cross-culturally.

5. Always agree to a few ground rules and procedures with your interpreter in advance. I typically remind him not to answer questions for me. I tell him to ask me for an explanation of

any jargon or idiomatic speech that I use if he's not positive he understands it. Experienced interpreters know such guidelines very well, and I can usually mention them quickly and move on. We also agree on logistics such as when we will take breaks.

6. If you deal with difficult or sensitive topics, such as ethics issues, ask the interpreter not to "sanitize" your message or to revise it to be culturally or politically correct. Sometimes when discussing a difficult topic (such as rape, murder, racism, or Nazi Germany), I have explained to the listeners (through the interpreter) that what we are about to discuss is difficult to talk about and may even be difficult for the interpreter to translate, but these are my own words, not the interpreter's. A good interpreter accurately represents what you, the speaker, are saying. Imagine the legal and ethical complications of a doctor announcing to a patient that she has a terminal illness and the interpreter "softens" the message so that death and the disease are not directly mentioned.

Agreeing in advance on ground rules and principles such as these helps avoid confusion and communication breakdown. To use an interpreter who has not been briefed or who is unqualified, biased, or unprepared is asking for trouble. Trust in your interpreter is critically important.

Target Country Knowledge

In addition to the ideas and frameworks for understanding culture presented earlier in this book, the suggestions I made earlier in Part 6 based on the five culture scales, and the various communication skills discussed above, there are three broad directions which I recommend you explore to increase your cultural intelligence. In the next few pages I will very briefly touch on these categories and why I think they are important. But these categories and quick suggestions are only intended as a starting point. It's up to you to find relevant material relating to the specific cultures that are appropriate to your situation.

Historical Overview

Modern-day culture in every world region has been shaped by its history. Whether you plan to live and work abroad or interact with international professionals at home, the more you know about your foreign counterparts' country, the better.

Let's say that you plan to work with Asians. How has Chinese culture affected Singapore, Malaysia, Korea, Japan, and Indonesia? How is Singapore, for instance, related to Malaysia? Was it ever politically a part of Malaysia? Do the two countries have a good relationship? What aspects of history have led to conflict between Taiwan and China? Is Taiwan really part of China? Can the residents of both places travel freely

Why do certain parts of the world fit together, while others don't?

from one to the other? And most important, what kinds of questions about Taiwan can get you into hot water in China? Or vice versa.

Why might it be important to have a basic knowledge about your international counterparts' history? It's a basic courtesy, for starters. Citizens in most countries care deeply about their history. They will respect you far more if you've made the effort to learn at least some of the most important historical themes, events, and heroes: colonization, immigration patterns, rulers and leaders of the past and present, wars and occupations, languages and lifestyles. Don't allow yourself to be labeled as yet another ignorant American.

Economic System

Basic economics is also important. For example, what are the main industries in the country you deal with? Who are the major trading partners in the region or world? Does the country tend toward high-tech or low-tech production? What is a "livable wage"? At what age do people retire? Is the country economically protectionist, or does it welcome foreign investment? What is the gap between rich and poor? Up to what level does the national government pay for education? What percentage of the population has a computer or at least access to the Internet? Is health care free? Can only the rich afford cars? How have the markets of the country performed over the last several years? Is it easy to be an entrepreneur in the target country, or are there significant barriers? Does bankruptcy usually mean one failed business initiative that can be followed by a chance to start again, or will it result in long-lasting family shame and a loss of face? To what degree do the people emphasize conspicuous consumption and consumerism?

You should be aware of economic issues because they determine, directly or indirectly, a wide range of issues such as market opportunities, business beliefs and practices, a propensity to live to work or work to live, hiring practices, company loyalty, willingness of employees to relocate, attitudes toward elitism or equality, and so forth.

Social Structure and Ethnicity

Attitudes toward elitism or egalitarianism lead me to a third vital aspect of knowing about a country or region: social and ethnic patterns. Take Australia, for example. The white Australians originally came to their island as deported convicts, and the local aboriginal population was decimated by disease and warfare. Today, some of the white Australians feel invaded by Asians, and protectionist movements aimed at stopping immigration have been the result. It just wouldn't be right for you to set foot (or open your mouth during a dinner conversation) on Australian soil without knowing something about these social and ethnic aspects of Australian history and the various views resulting from it.

Even if it's not important to you personally, include religion in your study because it may be very important to the people with whom you will interact. In Saudi Arabia, for example, there is no separation of church and state (this is also true in Pakistan, Yemen, and Iran). Islamic law (Sharia) cannot be dismissed as unimportant. Prayer schedules five times a day are taken seriously in some Muslim-dominated countries. You will want to be sensitive to these required breaks and respectful.

Are men's and women's roles drastically different? How do people dress? Is there a dress code you should follow? Are there laws you need to know about? Upon entering some countries, you must sign a form acknowledging that you are aware that the penalty for drug convictions is death—this is both a social statement and a legal one, but I have signed such statements and have never wanted to try to find out if or how they are enforced.

What are the different ethnic groups in the country? Which is dominant and why? Do races and ethnic groups mix? Are any groups discriminated against? Do people marry across race and ethnic lines? Which regions are populated by the various groups? How can you easily identify the regions people are from (and is it useful to do so)? Does class structure appear to be rigid or fluid? Are there sharp distinctions among classes?

Such issues as race, ethnicity, and class structure are important because you will need to fit in; you will also need to know how others will perceive you and interact with you if they are coming to your country. In some ways, social status may not be seen as very important in the United States, but in other places it is taken quite seriously—in India and Britain, for example. Many of the African immigrants and students I have known in the U.S. are sons, daughters, or relatives of African leaders, deposed presidents, or royal families.

I have mentioned what might seem like a laundry list of questions for each of the three categories above and described why I think they can be important. I encourage you to see my questions as merely examples of starting points for further exploration.

When researching any of the above three categories, I recommend that you watch for "hot button" issues you might want to avoid, such as class in England, Israel in Arab countries, the English in Ireland, the American military in Korea (and many other places), and so on. Find out from a trusted local what any such hot buttons might be. And be prepared to have your own hot buttons pressed while you are abroad. If you haven't noticed, Americans (and especially American foreign policy) are perceived negatively in many countries and areas. I think that others have perfectly legitimate and understandable reasons for criticizing the United States for historical, political, economic, and social reasons. I don't mean to sound preachy, but when faced with such criticism, I feel that honest exploration and genuine attempts at understanding others' views are good first steps toward open-mindedness and are an important aspect of increasing your cultural intelligence.

International Ethical Issues

In this final section of Part 6 I want to touch on the issue of ethics, and present to you a simple framework for dealing with the complexities of ethical choices in your work with people from other cultures.

The reason I close the book with a section on ethics is because, as you have certainly seen by now, cultural differences result in myriad ways of perceiving the world. People of all cultures have firmly held beliefs, attitudes, and values that result in significantly different behaviors, such as business practices and workplace behaviors, and this book has examined many of these. Cultural differences necessarily lead to conflicts. At some time, every internationally focused professional will be faced with potentially difficult decisions. Because of this, the ability to operate within an ethical framework is a necessary component of cultural intelligence.

A typical ethical dilemma might be an American dealing with a Chinese distributor who hires relatives and family members in spite of having explicitly agreed not to do so in a signed contract. The American attaches great value to the signed contract and needs to enforce a central policy to be fair to other distributors, but the Chinese distributor needs to look out for family and relatives first and places less emphasis on the written contract. Or an American company is prevented by policy and/or law (such as the Foreign Corrupt Practices Act) from accepting "bribes," but what we perceive as bribes are part of doing business in a particular country. These types of clashes illustrate the difficulties that arise when the home policy must be enforced across international borders.

In suggesting ways you can respond to ethical situations that you may encounter, I will offer a simple model you can use for facing actual situations in a meaningful way.

Here's my disclaimer: I said at the beginning of Part 6 that in this section I want to focus on what you can *do*, what *practical actions* you can take to increase your cultural intelligence. But I want to offer a disclaimer before I make these final comments on ethics. I am by no means in a position to offer any legal (or ethical) advice in my comments below about what you can *do*. Instead, I only want to raise some questions for you and to offer you a practical way of grappling with issues you may face now or in the future. What you ultimately decide to *do* about an ethical issue is entirely up to you. It's usually pretty easy to tell if something is legal or illegal in the larger picture. Robbing a bank, for example, is something that most people would immediately understand to be illegal and unethical. Giving money to a charity is something most people would recognize as both legal and ethical.

Written laws offer relatively clear guidelines for each, but there is a lot of "gray" space to consider, and here is where ethics takes center stage. Most people define *ethical* as what is good or right or fair or sometimes just normal or commonly accepted.

One person's perception of a good, fair, or normal business practice, however, may be seen by another as completely unfair or even corrupt. This is especially true for people who are doing business across international boundaries, where one's own sense of ethics may not fit. In other words, cultural context determines what is right and what is wrong.

For example, in North America bribery is an illegal activity, and corporations even have strict limits on gift giving. It is considered unfair if a company gives a large gift to another company and then receives something in return, such as a lucrative contract. In some other countries, quite the opposite may be true; gift giving and reciprocity may ethically be the standard way of doing business. A company may indeed be *expected* to give a gift if it is bidding for a contract. Where gift giving is a normal part of business, it is not seen as wrong or unethical.

Here's another example of ethical perceptions: nepotism. Hiring a family member or close friend for a well-paid position in a company is strongly discouraged in the United States. A job is likely to be filled (at least in theory) through the selection of a candidate according to résumés, scores on skill tests, past work experience, and so forth. Such hiring practices are considered fair and impartial—to people in the United States. In many other parts of the world, family comes first. Brothers and sisters, cousins, or very good friends can be trusted and therefore are most often hired over candidates with superior qualifications. This practice is not considered corrupt, wrong, or unethical. In

It's 2:00 a.m. You're at a deserted intersection with no other cars for miles. The light is red. Is it legal to go through it? Is it ethical? Would you have already gone through it in the time it took to read this?

those cultures where commitment to family and to established relationships comes first, being impartial or impersonal is irrelevant.

These are culture-based ethical differences, and some U.S. executives become quite frustrated when they cannot enforce typical U.S. policies overseas.

As is commonly done with two themes occupying opposite poles, let's divide the concepts of ethics and legality into four intersecting quadrants. Below are some examples (generated by my graduate students) of activities that might go in these four quadrants.

	Ethical	Unethical
Legal	Quadrant 1. (Legal and Ethical) • Donating to charity	Quadrant 2. (Legal and Unethical) • Restricting immigration?
Illegal	Quadrant 3. (Illegal and Ethical) • Medicinal marijuana?	Quadrant 4. (Illegal and Unethical) • Robbing a bank

I put question marks by the items in Quadrants 2 and 3 because not everyone would agree with these categorizations.

In which quadrant would you put gift giving to obtain a contract, as in our example above? Or what about nepotism? In the United States, we consider gift giving illegal and unethical (Quadrant 4) and nepotism, unethical but legal (Quadrant 2). Mexicans find nothing unethical about hiring family members in their businesses. In fact, businesses there are often structured much like a family enterprise. Mexicans may well put this type of nepotism in Quadrant 1. Similarly, the Chinese consider gift giving and reciprocal obligation as normal and would probably choose Quadrant 1 for those practices.

I actually did have one client, for example, whose Chinese distributors persisted in including family members in their distributorships even though this practice was explicitly prohibited in the legal contract they had signed. For the Chinese, family came first, and since there was nothing perceived as wrong about that, the legal contract itself took a distant second place in importance. The Chinese understood that they were violating the legal contract, so in this case, they would have put nepotism in Quadrant 3: illegal according to the American paperwork but ethical according to the Chinese way. (I encouraged my client to seek legal advice from both Chinese and American attorneys specializing in this area and focused my own consulting efforts on how the client might avoid such misunderstandings in the future through a better understanding of Chinese practices and clearer communication.)

The following list shows some items that might fall in various quadrants of the ethical/unethical, legal/illegal table from the previous page. In which quadrant would you place each item?

Every one of the items in the list will be perceived differently by members of various cultures. I recommend using or adapting this table for team discussions on ethics. If you or your team perceive the business practices of others as *wrong*, you may need to reconsider them within the context of a specific culture. It's also important to realize that your own business practices, which you may take for granted, may indeed be negatively perceived elsewhere.

In summary, the combination of legal and ethical issues across international trade boundaries can indeed lead to many gray areas. The solution is to do your homework before you make initial contact. Learn as much about management and policy cross-culturally as you can. There are a number of good books that can help you (see Recommended Readings).

Insider dealing

Nepotism

Immigration policy—restricting immigration and emigration

Death penalty

War

Burning your own music CDs from files downloaded from the Internet

Women voting

A fourteen-year-old buying wine at the supermarket to bring home to the family

Untested diet drugs available on the consumer market

Prostitution

Child labor

Treatment of animals in research or as pets

Unsafe building codes

Bribery in government road building or railway projects

Using information without citing the source

Whistling at a pretty woman in the street

Bribes

Separating men and women in the office

Women not being allowed to drive

Not respecting contracts

Selling cigarettes to seventeen-year-olds

An entire MBA class photocopying a university textbook instead of purchasing it

Women wearing veils for religious purposes

Costly military spending

Selling technology that can be used in harmful ways

Workplace safety standards

Dishonesty or exaggeration in advertising

Making false medical claims

Allowing people to choose where they want to live

Spitting your chewing gum on the sidewalk

Driving a car after having had three or four drinks

Going through a red light at 2:00 a.m. when no other cars are coming

Having a picture of nude women on a screen saver in the office

Prison policies

Possible "Translations" for Tip 1, page 191

Making the most of your English:

- We need a level playing field.
  We need things to be fair.

- This project is a strikeout.
  This project will not work.

- Let me run this idea past you.
  Let me tell you my idea.

- That plan has been sidelined.
  That plan has been postponed.

- Am I in the ballpark?
  Am I right/accurate/close?

- We're dealing with a SNAFU here.
  This (project) is full of mistakes/problems.

- Joe really shoots from the hip.
  Joe doesn't plan carefully.

- Fire off a memo to Silvana.
  Quickly send a letter to Silvana.

- There is no magic bullet.
  There is no universal solution.

Afterword

Some people might feel that in order to attain a desirable level of cultural intelligence you have to have lots of years of experience traveling or living overseas, a job in a major global corporation, a business card with an important international job title, a high IQ, and an address in a major city with lots of exposure to people from all around the world. The thinking seems to go that if you *have* these kinds of things, plus lots of stamps in your passport, you'll *be* culturally intelligent.

My experience tells me that this thinking is false.

I would suggest to you that rather than thinking about what titles and credentials you have, it's better to commit to being culturally intelligent and then plan ways of getting there. This will put you leagues ahead of someone who merely has the stamps in the passport and the fancy business cards.

And achieving cultural intelligence does not happen overnight. Nor is cultural intelligence ever finite; you can always learn more. It's normal to be occasionally frustrated with any process involving learning or evolution.

So I encourage you to commit to increasing your cultural intelligence and to realize that it will take years. Those years can be pleasant if you enjoy the process. Like the patient bonsai hobbyist who loves the slow process of growing his miniature trees, you can enjoy the process of increasing your cultural intelligence.

Appendix

Across Cultures Online Tools

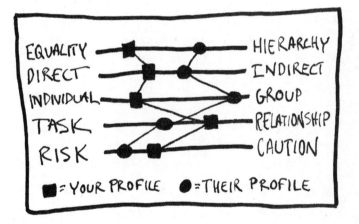

Across Cultures, offers a variety of online tools that have helped thousands of internationally focused professionals improve their dealings with people from other cultures.

The Peterson Cultural Style Indicator™ was developed to offer professionals an understanding of the important cultural and international business-related issues. It offers a quick and reliable way of helping people first understand their cultural style and then compare their style with what is typically expected in any of 60+ target countries (e.g., Brazil, China, Germany, Japan, etc.). Your answers are computer scored, and you will instantly see a personalized profile. Each profile shows

- a description of the five global culture scales discussed in this book,
- where you ranked on the five culture scales,
- where the target culture ranks on the same scale, and
- a description of how you might strategically improve based on how the profiles mix.

This tool is recommended as a companion to the discussions and insights in *Cultural Intelligence*. The online tool offers you a research-validated, accurate measurement of your own culture-based values and attitudes (along with specific suggestions for how you might change your behaviors to be more effective), and this book in turn offers deeper insights on the five culture themes and the process of increasing your cultural intelligence based on your cultural profile.

Sample items are listed below.

1. You are a new employee in a large organization. After a few days on the job you have an idea for increasing the overall profit of the organization. Will you tell your manager about this idea?

0	1	2	3	4	5	6	7	8	9	10

Probably not—because it's a manager's job to think about these things.

Probably yes—because any employee who has a good idea should be listened to.

2. During a discussion in a team meeting, a young member of the team has a viewpoint that is very different from what the older director is saying. In your opinion, what should the young team member do?

0	1	2	3	4	5	6	7	8	9	10

He or she should respect the director's authority and not challenge the director's view-point.

He or she should confront the director by offering a different viewpoint.

3. A plant manager calls a meeting and makes a brief presentation to the workers on the need to increase productivity. How will you interpret this message from the plant manager?

0   1   2   3   4   5   6   7   8   9   10

Based on how it was said— the manager's manner and style, tone of voice, level of dress, formality, etc.

Based on what was said—for example, the main points the plant manager communicated.

---

4. You will be meeting someone from another company to discuss issues and potential problems relating to an upcoming technology exchange program between your two companies. How will you prefer to proceed in the talks?

0   1   2   3   4   5   6   7   8   9   10

Remain respectful and diplomatic, avoiding disagreement when possible.

Have open, frank discussions of concerns and any issues that may arise.

---

5. You are in a group of employees who must carry out a project together. Given the choice, how will you, personally, want the group to work?

0   1   2   3   4   5   6   7   8   9   10

Harmony of the group is the key. A focus on the goals of the group will enable us to achieve more than if we emphasize our individual efforts.

Individual initiative is key. Each person needs to take initiative and work to achieve something unique and useful that will help.

---

6. How do you prefer to define yourself in the community where you live and work?

0	1	2	3	4	5	6	7	8	9	10

My identity is based on my family, friends, and by belonging to various groups.

Who people are: What issues interest them, how they describe themselves, what they feel is important, etc.

7. A business colleague is arriving for a weeklong visit to your headquarters. On his first day at headquarters, what will you, as the host, do together with him?

0	1	2	3	4	5	6	7	8	9	10

Pleasure before business: Welcome him, spend time making him feel comfortable and getting to know him, and later discuss business with him.

Business before pleasure: After the introductions, cover some basic business objectives first, then move on to more personal issues.

8. You are in a group of people your age (a mix of men and women) at a small company gathering and you have never met some of the people before. As you introduce yourself and get to know the others, what would you prefer to talk about more?

0	1	2	3	4	5	6	7	8	9	10

What people do: Where they work, what their job is, hobbies or activities they enjoy, etc.

Who people are: What issues interest them, how they describe themselves, what they feel is important, etc.

Further information on all of the Across Cultures online tools and associated consulting services is available at AcrossCultures.com

Recommended Readings

Books

Here is my short list of suggested resources to supplement cross-cultural training programs or to help you get started in your personal exploration of cultures.

All of the books below are culture general to some extent; none focuses solely on one particular culture, industry, or profession. These are books that I personally own and find useful. The descriptive comments about each book are my own, but some also reflect the feedback from my students and clients.

Adler, Nancy. 2002. *International Dimensions of Organizational Behavior*. Mason, OH: South-Western. This book does a good job of examining the international cultural dynamics of companies, teams, work groups, and so forth. I like it because it clearly and simply summarizes and applies the main ideas of Geert Hofstede, a major researcher and well-established name in the cross-cultural field.

Bartlett, Christopher, and Sumantra Ghoshal. 1998. *Managing across Borders: The Transnational Solution*. Boston, MA: Harvard Business School Press. Focuses on building innovation, flexibility, and coordination in transnational organizations. Includes case studies and organizational models and theories as they relate to international business.

Borden, George. 1991. *Cultural Orientation: An Approach to Understanding Intercultural Communication*. Englewood Cliffs, NJ: Prentice-Hall. Describes relevant communication codes and a variety of personal and cultural orientations that come into play in international mixes.

Bosrock, Mary Murray. 1990s. The Put Your Best Foot Forward series. St. Paul, MN: International Education Systems. These books come in several editions, one focusing on Asia, one on South America, one on Russia, and so forth. These guides list many anecdotes and lots of dos and don'ts. They are entertaining to read, but they are missing a solid theoretical foundation. Also recall my cautionary remarks on focusing too much on dos and don'ts. That said, I recommend them as an entertaining, introductory supplement to more significant material you will need to read on the countries you are interested in.

Gergersen, Hal, and Stewart Black. 1998. *So You're Going Overseas: A Handbook for Personal and Professional Success*. San Diego, CA: Global Business Publishers. This is a quick and light introductory overview of what people often face throughout the process of going on overseas assignments. I recommend it as an introductory reader to anyone going on extended international stays alone or with family members.

Gundling, Ernest. 2003. *Working GlobeSmart: 12 People Skills for Doing Business across Borders*. Palo Alto, CA: Davies-Black. This is a practical look at the skills necessary for international business success. It examines three progressively broader areas: interpersonal, group, and organizational skills. There are many useful illustrative cases. I recommend this book for both those who make and those who implement strategic international business decisions.

Hampden-Turner, Charles, and Fons Trompenaars. 2000. *Building Cross-Cultural Competence*. New Haven, CT: Yale University Press. Written by some of the biggest names in the cross-cultural field, this book contains interesting metaphors and anecdotes describing cultural differences. I've found that the rather abstruse writing style and confusing terminology can be a turn-off for many; it's certainly not light reading, but I recommend it because the book does offer deeper insights on national cultural differences and their impact on company strategy, work style, and so forth.

Hofstede, Geert. 1995. *Cultures and Organizations: Software of the Mind: Intercultural Cooperation and Its Importance for Survival*. New York: McGraw-Hill. An often referred-to classic. Loaded with numerical data describing Hofstede's research and illustrative cases describing his perceptions and approaches to culture and management.

Klopf, Donald. 1995. *Intercultural Encounters: The Fundamentals of Intercultural Communication*: Morton Publishing Company. A general, college-level primer on myriad issues such as the interplay of language, culture, beliefs, and behaviors in the communication process.

Koslow, Lawrence, and Robert Scarlett. 1999. *Global Business: 308 Tips to Take Your Company Worldwide*. Houston, TX: Gulf Professional Publishing. As the title suggests, there are 308 specific tips, based on cases discussing important cross-cultural considerations. These range from the issues facing one person being sent overseas to those facing a company strategically expanding into new international markets.

Morosini, Piero. 1999. *Managing Cultural Differences: Effective Strategy and Execution across Cultures in Global Corporate Alliances*. New York: Pergamon Press. This book looks at the important influences of national culture on corporate mergers and acquisitions, joint ventures, partnerships, and so forth. It uses illustrative cases and makes recommendations on how to avoid the many pitfalls of various international alliances.

Morrison, Terri, Wayne Conaway, and George Borden. 1994. *Kiss, Bow, or Shake Hands: How to Do Business in Sixty Countries*. Avon,

MA: Adams Media Corporation. This book offers business-people valuable practical tips for communicating with people in sixty countries. Based on a reasonable cultural framework explained briefly in the beginning of the book, it deals with each country in a half-dozen pages full of practical tips. I recommend this book as a resource for people who need a very quick overview of a number of countries.

Perry, Gaye, ed. 1999. *Perspectives: Intercultural Communications*: CourseWise Publishing. This college-level, large-format paperback is partly a workbook and largely a collection of cases and articles dealing with international, culture-focused issues such as negotiation, performance evaluation, and business protocols. The book does a good job of examining various concepts of culture and their implications.

Samovar, Larry, and Richard Porter. 2003. *Intercultural Communication: A Reader*. 10th ed. Belmont, CA: Wadsworth Publishing Company. This is a good theoretical textbook for understanding intercultural communication theory and I often use it in the graduate-school classes I teach. It's a collection of a few dozen academic papers exploring diverse intercultural communication issues. I recommend it as a fascinating work that offers good insights for the more academically minded.

Urech, Elizabeth. 1997. *Speaking Globally: How to Make Effective Presentations across International and Cultural Boundaries*. Dover, NH: Kogan Page. A good guide on a variety of issues relating to how culture affects both the way presentations are delivered and the way they are received. Topics include issues such as how to involve the audience, effective persuasion, and connecting with an international audience while avoiding improper use of humor. I have used this one as a text when teaching a class on effective international presentations.

Journals of Interest

Anthropological Journal on European Cultures. "A forum for social and cultural anthropologists working in Europe, presenting both new ethnographic work and more theoretical reflections on the history and politics of the field."

International Business Review. Relevant to both academics and businesspeople, this journal focuses on topics such as strategic planning, foreign investment, motivation, leadership, and management.

International and Intercultural Communication Annual. A scholarly journal examining the international cultural aspects of issues such as communication, cultural identity, sociology, and language.

International Journal of Intercultural Relations. A resource focused on intercultural topics, diversity, conflict avoidance, diplomatic relations on the interpersonal level, and so forth.

International Journal of Politics, Culture, and Society. Specializes in international women's issues and gender issues such as discrimination, employment rights, prostitution, and trafficking.

Journal of International Affairs. With a focus on the political, this journal looks at "heated debates in international affairs."

Journal of International Business Studies. Presents business-focused topics such as international expansion, strategic marketing, brand names across cultures, and international wage issues.

Management International Review. On topics relating to international business ventures such as job satisfaction and adjustment, adapting contracts to local conditions and practices, and the strategic rationale for international partnerships.

About the Author

Brooks Peterson founded Across Cultures, Inc., in 1997 after more than a decade in the cross-cultural arena. His experience includes offering programs and seminars to internationally focused professionals on countries in Europe, Asia and the Pacific Rim, the Middle East, Scandinavia, and the Americas.

Dr. Peterson has lived, worked, and traveled extensively overseas and has delivered products and services in a variety of settings inside and outside the United States to diverse clients in academic, business, manufacturing, nonprofit, and military fields.

Dr. Peterson has taught a variety of international management and communication topics in MBA programs in the Minneapolis area. He holds a B.A. in French, an M.Ed. in adult education, and a Ph.D. in Second Languages and Cultures.

To contact the author, or for further information on the products, seminars, and consulting services offered by Across Cultures. please visit: AcrossCultures.com

www.AcrossCultures.com